D0469171

DATING SMARTS

What Every Teen Needs to Know to Date, Relate or Wait!

By

Amy Lang, MA

ISBN-13: 978-1502439642
ISBN-10: 1502439646

For Kerry, Milo, my brother, my parents, my in-laws, and Margit. For my consultants - D. Z., G. W., B. Y., my editors, everyone who read early drafts, gave me helpful hints, and The Eastside Teen Peer Advocate Program aka the "wo-girls" at the Asian Counseling Referral Service in Bellevue, WA. And most especially, thanks to Arden for bringing the real world right to my doorstep.

Thanks for all of your advice, help and support!

Table of Contents

Introduction and Pop Quiz...8

Sexuality and Relationships 12
    Stuff to Think About!.. 15

Whose Values Count? Where Are You Coming From?.............. 17
    My Parents' or Family's Core Values........................... 19
    Get Clear! Get Savvy! Get Confident! 21
    A Handful of Value Issues to Consider 23

Impulsive You! Ack! What's Going On With
Your Teenaged Brain... 28
    The Power of "Maybe"... 31
    Sexting - The Impulse Trainwreck............................ 32
    Your Crazy Parents 34
    Stuff to Think About!.. 35

Romantic Love Versus Family Love: What's the difference? 36
    Love Really Shouldn't Hurt! 36
    Family and Friend Love... 37
    Romantic Love... 38
    What's the Difference? 40
    Guys and Sexuality... 40
    Girls and Sexuality 41
    What's the Benefit of Friends With Benefits and
    Hooking Up? 42
    Being in Love.. 43
    Stuff to Think About!.. 44

Are You Normal? Yeah, Most Likely............................... 46
    Who Do You Like? 47
    A Word About Sex, Gender and Transgender.................. 49
    Lust or Sexual Desire 50
    Pornography and You (or Amy Rants About Porn) 51

Stuff to Think About! 54

Wanna Go to the Movies? A Fake First Date 55
You Ask Someone Out! 56
Someone Just Asked You Out! 56
What to Do if You Don't Want to Date Them! 57
What to Do if You Want to Date Them! 58
Who's Going to Pay? 59
What Are You Going to Wear? 60
You're Out on the Date! 61
Should We Hold Hands or More? 63
The Date Is Over! 64
Post-date Assessment 65
You're Ready for Another Date! 66
Stuff to Think About! 66

Slow It Down or Speed It Up? Bumps in the Dating Road 67
Escape Plan 101 67
List of "Get Me Outta Here!" Situations 68
Deal Breakers: When It Might Be Time to
Dump Your Date 69
Pressure, Pressure, Pressure! 71
Intuition Is Your Friend 72
Dating Your Friends—Smart Move or Not? 73
Sex and Dating: The Two Most Important
Things to Know 74
Stuff to Think About! 75

Am I Really in Love? It's a Crush! It's Lust! It's Love! 76
Is It Lust? 78
Is It Love? 79
Sex, Again! 82
Sample Script to Get the "Sexual Communication"
Conversation Rolling 83
Stuff to Think About! 85

What's a Healthy Relationship? What You Should Expect..... 87

One Tip That May Just Be the Most Important Thing for You to Know!.. 87

Honest Communication 88

Respect and Thoughtfulness.. 89

Acceptance 90

Trust... 91

Boundaries... 91

Relationship Feelings.. 92

Good Relationship Feelings 93

Relationship Styles 94

List of Behaviors to Worry About 95

Stuff to Think About!... 98

When Should I End It? Signs to Know It's Time to Go............. 99

Dating Violence 99

The Cycle of Violence..102

How to Talk to Your Partner if They Do Something You Don't Like 104

Sexual Abuse 105

Talking about Sex in Your Relationship.........................107

Stuff to Think About!..108

Are You Ready for Sex? Part 1: The Emotional Stuff 109

The Longer You Wait, the Better the Sex!......................109

What the Heck Is "Sex" Anyway?.....................................110

How I Lost It! Tales about Losing Virginity 110

Gabe's Story—The Timing Felt Right 111

Katherine's Story—I Waited Until I Was Twenty-One.....112

Talia's Story—I Got It Over With 113

Julian's Story—It Was a Gift 114

Jessica's Story—I Was Engaged 114

Mathew's Story—I Was Drunk..115

Lillie's Story—I Was at Camp 116

Araceli's Story—I Found Out I Was a Lesbian 117

Kara's Story—I Did It with My First Love 119

Things to Think About Before You Have Sex 120

Pressure! 124

Not Ready? Here's Some Help. 125

Stuff to Think About! 126

Are You Ready For Sex? Part 2: The Physical Stuff 127

How Do You Know Your Vagina Is Healthy?* 128

How Do You Know Your Penis Is Healthy?* 130

STIs and HIV 132

Baby Away or Preg-NOT: Birth Control 134

Stuff to Think About! 138

Your Rules! What It Takes to Date You 139

How Will You Know When You Are Ready for Dating?... 140

Handy-dandy Dating Rules Checklists and Quiz 140

Parents and Dating 144

Stuff to Think About! 146

A Few Final Thoughts! 147

About the Author 148

Resources 151

End Notes 157

INTRODUCTION AND POP QUIZ

Pop quiz! Answer yes, no or maybe!

I feel confident and excited about dating and starting a romance.

I am ready for a sexual relationship.

I know and have thought about the qualities that are important to me in a boy or girlfriend.

I know my own values about dating, relationships, and sex.

I have been in love.

I am clear about my limits and how far I'll go with someone sexually.

I know the signs of trouble in a romantic relationship.

My parents have open and consistent conversations with me about dating, romance, and sex.

I have friends and other trusted people I can talk to about dating, romance, and sex.

I feel confident, smart, and ready for just about any dating or romantic situation.

Dating and relationships are two of the most confusing, complicated, crazy-making, fun, exciting, exhilarating, heartbreaking parts of life. This pop quiz is a way of getting you to think more clearly about how ready you are to dive into the sea of romance. How did you do? Did you learn anything when thinking about these questions?

My hope is that by reading this book and doing the exercises along the way, you will become a confident and smart dater. Of course, experience is the best teacher, but doing some preparation before you're out there will help things go more smoothly. You'll have a chance to test yourself again at the end.

Let's face it, figuring out the world of romance, dating, and sex is confusing! There is so much information coming at you all the time, it's hard to know what's accurate. Television, movies, magazines, the Internet, books, and video games are some of the main sources of messages about dating and relationships.

Since you are plugged into some kind of media pretty much all the time, these messages are fairly constant. Your friends also have many thoughts and opinions on this matter, as do your parents (whether or not they actually talk to you about them).

A lot of the information coming at you isn't even correct or based in reality. Sure, there are elements of reality—people really do meet and fall in love at first sight and are together from when they're fourteen until they are in their nineties. And, on the other end of the spectrum, many people do have casual sex with several different partners but they don't always come away feeling great about their choices.

Your friends may be dating and having sex and making it look like it's no big deal, when in fact, it really is a big deal to them. It's a crazy world out there and understanding it takes a little work.

Here's the deal. It's easy to get factual information about sex— how it all works, safe sex, birth control, sexually transmitted infections (STIs), HIV, even statistics about who is doing what and at what age. I include some of this information in this book. Your parents and friends are probably pretty good resources for some of this information, as is your healthcare provider and even the Internet if you know where to look. (There's a list of great sites in the Resources section at the end of the book).

The hard part of learning about dating, relationships, and sex is determining what it all means to you: Are you ready for it? How will you know? What do you believe about crushes, sexuality, dating, relationships, romance, falling in love, communication, and all that exciting and confusing stuff? Where do you stand? If you are religious, what does your religion say? Do you agree? What are your friends doing?

When you know your sexual values, which are what you believe to be true and right about these things, it makes it easier for you to:

- Make decisions you will look back on and feel great about

- Say "no" to stuff you're not ready for

- Be a great girlfriend or boyfriend

- Be supportive of your friends

- Feel really great about who you are in a relationship— be it romantic or otherwise

What about your parents? Talking about sexual values is the biggest thing parents can do for their teens. When teens know their parents' values, they make better decisions. Sadly, lots of parents don't talk openly to their kids about this. In the end, it's all up to you. No matter what, you need to figure out what your core beliefs are about sexuality, love, and relationships so you can confidently step into romance and dating.

Look at it this way - think about driving a car. You know your parents would not hand you a set of car keys and tell you "go for it!" on your sixteenth birthday without tons of guidance, practice, and lessons. Crazy, right? Well, sending you out into the world of dating and romance without guidance, information, and lots of support is just as crazy. My goal with this book is to help you get clear and feel confident and as ready as possible for this important part of life.

This book will serve as a "driver's manual" for you, as you develop your sexual values and learn the ropes of romance, dating, and sex. Remember, this book is for you and all about you. It's not for your parents, your friends, or the world at large. It's to help you get to know yourself better so you can one day confidently and consciously share your full self with another person.

Dating Smarts is really all about you and where you are in this very moment. Read it however it makes sense to you - complete it in one sitting or read it section by section. You might want to have a journal or paper available as you are reading so you can respond to questions and jot down your thoughts.

If you aren't sure about something, ask your parents or a trusted adult friend what they think—be bold! They really do want to help. Your friends can also be good resources, but remember, this is about you, not them. At the end of the book you'll also find great resources for getting more information or finding help if you need it.

CHAPTER ONE

Sexuality and Relationships: What's It All Mean, Anyway?

Let's start with some basic information about this thing called "sexuality." What the heck is it?

Being sexual is part of who we are as human beings—we are emotional, physical, intellectual, spiritual, and sexual from the moment of birth. It is a part of being human that we cannot and should not even try to escape.

It really is one of the coolest parts of being human because it sets us apart from the other animals, it drives our relationships and creates our families. We are pretty much the only animal that has sex for reproduction *and* mostly for fun. It is also something that can be very complicated and confusing. Everyone (and I mean *everyone*) finds sexuality challenging in some way.

Sexuality is everywhere you look: it's on TV, online, in video games, movies, music, commercials, and magazines. You think about it, your friends talk about it, and maybe your parents do, too. Being flooded with all this sex and sexuality and then be expected to act like you completely "get it" and are ready for anything can be a little overwhelming.

What does "sexuality" mean anyway? Maybe you've got it down and know what it is. Maybe you already have a great understanding of your own sexuality and are hopeful you will learn about someone else's someday soon. Or perhaps it's just another one of those words that you hear and kind of think you understand, but have never taken the time to really find out what it means.

Here's a dictionary definition of sexuality:

sex-u-al-i-ty [seks - shoo - AL- i - tee]—noun

Sexual character; having the structural and functional traits of sex, like being male or female. Making note of or highlighting sexual matters.

Involvement in sexual activity.

Being ready for engaging in sexual activity, which includes things like being physically ready, emotionally ready, having birth control and condoms, etc.

Let's break this down into the parts that probably have more meaning for you.

Making note of or highlighting sexual matters. This means noticing things related to sex. This could mean the act of sex itself, body differences, sexual practices, sexual orientation, language, even dating and romance.

Involvement in sexual activity. Obviously, this refers to the physical things that are involved in being sexual or having sex. There are lots of ways to be sexual with someone and include anything from hand holding to intercourse and everything in between and beyond.

Being ready for engaging in sexual activity. This is about being physically and emotionally prepared for sex. Because humans have sex for pleasure (99.9% of the time), and since there are some really big consequences from having sex, there's a bit more preparation that needs to go into it other than being physically mature and ready. This can include, among other things, being emotionally mature, which means you are ready to handle the consequences of your actions, talking to your partner about it, and confidently getting (and using) birth control and condoms.

At its core, sexuality is something private—even though you wouldn't think so by watching TV or surfing the web for an hour or two. Being bombarded with something that is ultimately very personal and constantly getting messages about what "should" be important, makes it confusing to try to figure out what truly matters to when it comes to sex and relationships.

You have probably felt a physical feeling, maybe like a rising surge through your body when you see someone you have a crush on. This is called sexual desire and it is part of a person's sexuality. You might have wondered: What the heck is going on?! Now that you've been in your body for a while, you are most likely familiar with this feeling.

Not to worry if you haven't experienced this—it'll probably happen to you eventually. You'll see a cute guy or girl and zing! there's that good feeling of sexual desire. Not everyone experiences sexual desire – this is pretty rare, and this is called being asexual and is totally normal, too.

Sex feels good and it's supposed to be because our main biological drive behind sex is to reproduce. Nature figured that if it wasn't fun we might not do it enough and then —no more humans! Clearly this isn't a problem—there are plenty of people reproducing and plenty more just "practicing."

Relationships Are Like The Container For Sexual Activity

You can't have any kind of sexual activity with someone without having a relationship with that person, even if it's a casual, like the—usually unsuccessful— idea of "friends with benefits" or "hooking up." This is when people who are "just friends" have sex for fun, but aren't actually involved in a romantic relationship. This can be disastrous: someone's feelings nearly always get hurt.

The relationship within which (this is why I used the word "container") you have sex may be very serious, such as with the first person you fall in love with. It may be a relationship with someone you like and are dating, but don't know if you really love them or ever will. Or it can be a completely casual event, with someone you barely know. There are many different kinds of relationships that include sex.

It may seem like everyone you know has already had sex but you. This just isn't true. Most studies show that about half of teenagers have had sex. Clearly, this isn't everybody, but when you haven't had sex and the whole world makes a big deal out of who's doing it and who isn't, it can feel like you are the only person on the planet who hasn't. (Don't worry. You aren't!).

Or maybe you have had sex and feel really confident about your relationships, dating, and your choices. Either way, giving some thought to what's going on around you can help you become clearer about what's true for you.

No matter what, it's important for you to be really clear about who you are and what your values are, so you can be a great partner to someone—whether now or in the future. The more information you have about yourself, being safe, healthy relationships, and everything that can go along with dating—your sexual values— the happier you will be with your choices. We'll talk more about these in the next chapter.

Stuff to Think About!

What are some of the media messages you get about sex and relationships?

What other "sexual matters" can you think of? What does this bring to mind?

How do you define "the bases"—the steps or levels of sexual

activity?

What do you think you need to be prepared to have sex?

What kinds of romantic relationships are your friends involved in? Do they seem healthy to you? If these relationships involve sex or sexual activity, what are your feelings about this?

CHAPTER TWO

Whose Values Count? Where Are You Coming From?

When you know, understand, and can talk about your values, including your sexual values, you'll make better decisions. Just the act of giving thought and voice to what you believe helps you stand firm in the face of situations that might not be good for you in the long run.

Values are core beliefs that have a degree of emotional investment. It's the emotional connection to your values that makes them truly your own. If you don't connect to something emotionally, you may have a much harder time sticking to your values when it's really important.

Because this is a book about dating, relationships, and sex, we'll be focusing on values related to relationships and sexuality. Some of these values are also values people hold in other parts of their lives, but I want you to think about these values as they relate to dating and relationships.

Core sexual values are what you believe to be fundamentally important and true for you about relationships, dating, sex, and sexuality. Your sexual values can be influenced by your religion, your politics, your culture, your experiences, the messages you receive from your family and friends, and your own emotional connection.

Here is why knowing your core values about dating, relationships, romance, sex, and sexuality is important: they act as a guide to help you make decisions that you can feel good about. Consider your core values to be a map of sorts. It's really hard to get someplace you've never been without any directions. You might have the street address and know the city, but without a map or some kind of guide, it'll take you a long time to get there.

If you're lucky, you'll end up where you intended, but if not, you may end up in a place that is on the opposite side of the world. Clarifying your values is a simple thing you can do that will help you feel confident and proud of your choices and decisions—in all aspects of your life.

Because values, and sexual values in particular, are such a personal thing, it's hard to tell someone what to believe. Your parents and other adults in your life are communicating their values to you all the time. They may not speak openly about them, but if you think about it and pay attention to the things they buy, the television shows they watch, the books they read, their religion, who they vote for, the comments they make about the world around them, you will notice that they have been communicating with you about their values all along.

You may be in a family that talks about values openly and consistently and maybe even about sexual values. Or maybe you are in a family that doesn't spend much time communicating about anything, ever. Either way you are developing your own values and your family has been an influence on you.

When you were younger, you would listen, watch, and take all this in without much question. Now that you are older and have been on the planet for a while, you are developing your own opinions about what is true for you. You may not always agree with your parents' or caregivers' perspectives. This is part of what being a teenager and the process of becoming an adult is all about separating from your parents and family.

Start thinking about your family's or parents' core values regarding sex and relationships. Following you'll find a big list of values. If you look at this list and have little or no idea what your family's values are, think about societal values— what have you learned about sexual values from the media, religion, friends, and our culture.

My Parents' or Family's Core Values about Relationships, Dating, and Sex

What are the top ten you think, or know, apply to your family's or parents' belief system when it comes to sex and relationships.

- Being yourself

- Caring
- Happiness

- Commitment
- Health

- Communication
- Honesty

- Confidence
- Integrity

- Courage
- Kindness

- Dependability
- Knowledge

- Empathy
- Listening

- Fairness
- Love

- Faith
- Loyalty

- Family
- Others first

- Generosity
- Passion

- Gratitude
- Patience

- Peace

- Perseverance

- Preparation

- Reputation

- Respect

- Responsibility

- Safety

- Self-confidence

- Self-respect

- Sex is a great part of life

- Sex is for later

- Sex is for marriage

- Sex is for when you are "ready"

- Sharing

- Truth

Now, thinking about sex and relationships, go back through the list and pick out the top five values you think best represent your family's core values. You might want to write them down. Any surprises?

Okay, now it's your turn! Go back through the list and pick out the top five you think best represent your core values. Write them down next to your family's core values. Any surprises?

Next, take a moment and compare your values and your family's values? What stands out for you? Do they feel balanced? You may find that your values and your family's values are different and this is okay. Remember you need to respect their values even if you don't agree with them, just like you want them to respect your values even if they don't agree with them.

Take some time to break down and think about each of your core values. As an example, what does "trust" mean to you? How do you know someone is trustworthy? How do you know someone is untrustworthy? If trust is important to you, but you don't really know what it means, or have any concrete examples of trust in relationships, how will you know when you are experiencing it? We'll be looking at this value really closely in just a bit.

Making a list of what's important to you in a relationship based on your values will make dating and romance a lot easier. Starting a romantic relationship is confusing—no matter how old you are! Both people wonder if the other person "likes" them. Both wonder if the relationship will "go anywhere." Both wonder, "What will my friends/family/parents think of this person?"

Understanding what's important to you before you start dating someone (or even if you are already dating someone) will save you quite a bit of heartache. You can use your values like a checklist to help you understand both yourself and the other person.

Get Clear! Get Savvy! Get Confident!

When you think more deeply about your core values, break them down, and get clear about what you will and will not put up with, you will have a really good understanding of what's important to you in your relationships. The end result? You will feel like a rock star of the dating world. Well, maybe not quite a rock star, but you'll feel tons more confident and all rock stars are confident, right?

Think about friends you have who are in unhealthy relationships. Their boyfriends or girlfriends control them, they build their world around their partners, stop hanging out with you, and maybe even start acting like someone you don't know. Trust me, you really don't want to be "that" guy or gal. Frankly, you'll just end up looking like an ass and your friends may not be so friendly when you come crawling back to them after the relationship ends. One way to prevent this is to take the time to get to know yourself, your wants and needs and

21

what's truly important to you in a relationship.

Let's take a deeper look and dig into one of the values that is most important in all relationships - trust. Trust is something that needs to grow and develop, because getting to know the other person requires time. Sometimes, you might think someone is trustworthy because of the stories you've heard about them, their reputation, or because they just "seem" trustworthy. This isn't always the most reliable way to decide if someone is worthy of your trust.

Say you text someone and ask them out and they agree. You decide on the date, time, and place and think you are off and running. You show up, they don't. No text, no call, no any-thing. They're just not there. How's your trust level? You text them and they get back to you with some excuse. You make another date and this time they show up!

Now, you feel a little better about their trustworthiness. Say this cycle continues, sometimes they show up when they say they will, sometimes they don't. You can't quite tell what's go-ing on or know if they will do what they say they will do. You probably don't fully trust them and feel a little uneasy about their trustworthiness.

If you tend to be the person who is unreliable and don't show up when you say you will, what does this say about you? How is this impacting your trustworthiness? What are people thinking about you? If this scenario rings a bell with you in your current or past relationship, what's the trust level?

I hope this has helped you understand what I mean by "breaking down your core values" so you can have a better understanding of what's important to you in your relation-ships. The more time you spend thinking and talking about your core values the better.

This exercise is intended to get you looking closely into your belief system. Some of your core values may be more about being ready for sex, others may be more about being in a relationship. By thinking about your sexual values, you have made big strides towards making great decisions. It might seem weird that something so small can make a difference, but it really can.

A Handful of Value Issues to Consider

We've talked about core sexual and relationship values and now it's time to spend a little time thinking about some big issues related to sexuality. These topics are things that are of real concern to teenagers (and everyone else, really) and, once again, the clearer you are about where you stand, the easier it will be for you if you are confronted with one of these situations in real life.

Topics like teen pregnancy, casual sex, and same sex relationships are situations or events that engage and sometimes even challenge our core beliefs. What we believe to be true for ourselves can be put to the test when we're faced with a situation that has many sides, perspectives, people, and even values related to it. Even a situation that isn't as challenging as these can teach you something about sexual and relationship values.

For example, Nate and Alison had been dating for about three weeks. However, Nate had a long time crush on Jenna, but always thought she wasn't interested in him. One afternoon, Nate ran into Jenna at the mall and, one thing lead to another and they ended up hanging out and holding hands.

Jenna, it turned out, was totally into Nate but didn't know that he was dating Alison. He didn't want to hurt Alison's feelings by breaking up with her, and he wasn't sure where things would go with Jenna, so he decided he would sneak around with Jenna until he could figure it out.

23

Alison figured out what was going on and immediately broke up with Nate, after giving him a piece of her mind. She was hurt and angry, and Nate felt like a giant . . . well, you know how he felt. And Jenna broke up with him as well because he wasn't the kind of person she thought he was—honest and full of integrity.

What if this happened to you and the person you are dating sneaks around behind your back and goes out with someone else? Maybe some of your core values about relationships are loyalty, honesty, and respect. Their decision to go behind your back goes against these core values and you would probably feel hurt and angry. You would also have some information about your girlfriend or boyfriend—maybe their values aren't the same as yours.

This is an example of how your values about sex and relationships can be used as a road map to guide you along the dating path. You can think about those moments when something goes against your value system like speed bumps, potholes, roadblocks, or a giant blinding blizzard, depending on the size of the problem. Basically, they are warning signs and you really should pay attention to them.

Sometimes, our friends do a better job of noticing this stuff than we do, so you might want to check in with a friend if you're wondering if you should be worried. They'll tell you the truth.

To help you learn more about your values, spend some time thinking about the following issues and, as you go through each one, ask yourself "What is right for me? What do I believe to be true?" Use the list of values and think about or jot down a couple related to the specific issue and then think or write about your response.

- Teen Pregnancy—Thoughts and reactions? What

would you do if you were involved in a pregnancy right now?

- Abortion—Pro or con? Do you believe abortion should be an option for women?

- Masturbation—Healthy or not healthy? It's completely normal to masturbate and completely normal not to masturbate, for both sexes. What do you think?

- Sex before marriage—Okay or not okay? What are the benefits to waiting? What are the benefits of not waiting?

- Sexually transmitted infections (STIs) and HIV—What's your plan? What do you know about transmission, signs, symptoms? What more do you want to know?

- Same sex relationships—Okay or not? Why do you believe this?

- Oral sex—Casual or intimate? With guys? With girls?

- Hooking up and Friends with benefits—Okay or not okay? Remember, it's still a relationship, even if it is casual.

- Multiple partners? Healthy exploration or risky behavior?

Clarifying your sexual values goes a long way towards helping you have healthy, fun, and great relationships. Whether you've never been on a date or have been on three hundred, knowing your beliefs will give you an advantage compared to most of the people you will be dating. If you feel clear about your values, you will be more confident, empowered, attractive and will be less likely to make decisions you regret later.

25

Stuff to think about!

How does your current relationship measure up to your core values?

Did your previous relationship match your values?

What about your friends' relationships? Does it seem like they are in relationships that go along with their values?

What's important to you about clarifying your values about sexuality and romance?

How does it feel when you go against your values?

Mini Rant About . . . Oral Sex!

People who tell you "oral sex isn't really sex" and isn't a big deal, are just plain wrong. Oral sex is, well, sex! It seems silly to have to point this out, but oral sex is a sexual act—no matter if anyone tells you differently. Just to be clear, oral sex is when one person puts their mouth on another person's penis or vaginal area for pleasure. When it's given to a guy it's called a blowjob, giving head, dome, or brain. When it's given to a woman it's called going down on her, muff diving, dining at the Y, or eating out.

You can get several things from oral sex: pleasure, sure, but also herpes, HIV, gonorrhea, or HPV in your vagina, penis, anus, mouth, or throat; and sometimes a bad reputation and feelings of low self-worth.

If you're thinking "I'm in charge! It's my decision!" or "She offered! She's willing!" this may indeed be the case, but if one of your sexual values is "respect," think about how accepting an offer of oral sex from someone you aren't in a romantic relationship with or aren't planning to return the favor for isn't respectful. Ideally, this is an intimate act that should be part of an intimate, not casual, relationship. Seriously, would you want your sister or your best friend doing this with just anyone?

If you offer oral sex to someone to get something from them or to prove something, think about how manipulative this is. Most people know that oral sex feels really, really good and they will have a hard time saying, "No thanks." Using oral sex in this way is disrespectful to the other person and to yourself.

Think seriously before you engage in casual oral sex - is it really worth the thrill?

CHAPTER THREE

Impulsive You! Ack! What's Going On With Your Teenaged Brain

Even though this might seem a bit out of place, the information in this chapter will make your life a little easier. You may have noticed that your parents are driving you crazy, you are more emotional than you used to be, and you sometimes do things without thinking them through. This last thing is called being impulsive, and, while fun, it can also get you into trouble.

Say "hello!" to your adolescent brain. Just as your body is going through some major changes, so is your brain. When you know what's going on with your brain, it will make it easier to deal with the times you have an "adolescent moment" such as doing something impulsive, emotional, or "crazy." This is not an excuse for your behavior, just an explanation.

Right after puberty starts at around eleven or so, when your body begins the process of changing from a child's body to an adult's, the brain begins a process of refining. The neural pathways of your brain that haven't been used much get trimmed away, and the parts that you use a lot get stronger. Think of this like a tune up or pruning a tree – branches that are important and supportive stay and the rest gets trimmed away.

One of the areas of your brain that gets tuned up is right behind your forehead, the prefrontal cortex. This part of your brain helps with:

- Impulse control

- Self-control

- Emotional control

- The ability to make good decisions

- Goal and priority setting

- Planning and organization of many tasks

While the prefrontal cortex is getting its tune up, it can't do a very good job of helping you out with things like controlling your urges or emotions. The part of the brain that's running the show at this time is the amygdale—the emotional center, which can make you, well, emotional. Sound familiar?

Here's an example of adolescent-brain-development induced craziness:

One morning Ella came downstairs for breakfast. Her mom looked at her and said, "Oh hey! Your hair looks different to-day!" Ella proceeded to completely freak out. She yelled, "You hate my hair! You think my hair looks terrible! I can't believe you'd say that to me!" She then burst into tears and ran up-stairs. Lovely way start to the day, right?

Ella, for whatever reason, completely misinterpreted what her mom said to her and blew her top! Her mom was totally baffled by Ella's behavior and sat there, mystified. Because Ella might have been feeling a little unsure that morning, tired, or even mad at her mom about something else and be-cause her prefrontal cortex was busy doing its tune up thing, her emotional center was front and center and ready to rock and roll. She freaked out over nothing.

Here's the deal—and the weird part—later that day Ella's mom said to her, "Remember this morning when you freaked out about your hair?" Ella responded "Huh? What are you talking about? I didn't freak out!" Sometimes after these moments, teens don't even remember that they went a little nuts.

You may never do this or you may do it all the time. The thing to remember is if you pay a little attention, you can feel the craziness coming on. Stop what you are doing and slowly count to ten. This will give you a chance to get your emotions under control before you say or do something you will regret. This will also help you learn to stay calm in the face of real danger.

As I mentioned, doing things without thinking them through first—being impulsive—can get you into trouble. While being impulsive isn't necessarily your "fault," it is your responsibility to be aware that you might have trouble considering the consequences of your actions. You need to do your best to take steps to at least try to give things some thought before you do them. From an evolutionary standpoint, there may be some important reason teens are impulsive, but it doesn't really serve the modern teenager.

What does this have to do with sex and dating? Your lack of impulse control can lead to jumping into sexual situations without thinking them through. This happens all the time. All. The. Time. I hope that by telling you about this, you may have a teeny-tiny bit more awareness and may be able to avoid impulsive decisions about sex.

Don't forget that you have also been given a big old dose of hormones. These hormones can also contribute to your, um, unstable behavior. Not to worry, however, everything will eventually calm down— your hormones will even out, your brain will make it through the development period, and you will settle down into your young adult self.

The Power of "Maybe"

When it comes to dating and sex, you can imagine the potential disaster if you're not quite able to think things through. It's a bit unfair that your brain is working against your ability to make thoughtful decisions, while at the same time Mother Nature is all for you getting out there and reproducing (or at least practicing).

What's a person to do? Well, as they say, knowledge is power. Or, as I prefer to say, knowledge is empowering. Understanding what is happening to you and why you sometimes do things without thinking them through is a big step toward slowing down and giving some thought before you make a decision.

One tip is to get in the habit of saying "maybe" when someone asks you to do something like go on a date, to a party, or any other situation you should give some thought. This is the easiest path to "no" as the person is already prepared to hear "no" without you actually saying it. This will buy you some time to thoughtfully consider your options and give you the space to construct your "no" if it's something you definitely don't want to do, like go on a date with that creepy guy or gal from your English class.

Practice saying "maybe" to something non-sexual so you can test it out and get used to using this tip. See what happens. Most people can live with "maybe" for a little while and you will feel much better about your decisions. You could say:

"Thanks for asking! I need to check my schedule/with my parents/think about it, so I'll say 'maybe' for now and get back to you."

"I'm not sure, so let me get back to you."

When it comes to sexual activity and if you're in the heat of the moment, "maybe" shouldn't be on your list of responses. It will be confusing to your partner and could result in a situation with which neither of you will be happy. If you're not sure, or are even a little bit uncomfortable with the way things are going, say "no" and stop what you're doing immediately.

Remember: if you say "maybe" you must say "yes" or "no" eventually, so be prepared with your answer. It's not nice or fair to leave someone hanging— especially if they have a crush on you. Put yourself in their shoes.

Saying "maybe" can help you stay true to your values and this can be very empowering and make you feel good about yourself. Feeling great and empowered is really attractive to other people because you will radiate confidence. Think of someone you know who may not be super attractive, but has "something" about them—they probably glow with confidence.

Sexting - The Impulse Trainwreck

One other little thing you may or may not take part in is "sexting" —sending text messages that are pictures of your naked body, private body parts or even just sexy pictures. Usually, people send texts on impulse because it seems like a cool or funny thing to do. What can be the harm? No one but the person who receives it will know! Ha! I know you know this is total BS because at this point you have probably either sent one yourself or seen someone else's.

Making, owning or sending sexual or sexy pictures of anyone under the age of 18 is considered child pornography and is illegal. Right now, the laws in the US haven't caught up to technology and as a minor, you can get into really big trouble if you send, keep or forward a sexual picture of yourself or anyone else.

My friend Jo Langford, author of *Spare Me the Talk* (an amazing sex ed book for guys), says "Felony. Felony. Felony." It's a felony to make the picture, to send it and to possess it. I like to add "forever, forever, forever" to this list.

Don't believe for one second that if you send a picture like this of yourself to someone you know and trust that it won't be forwarded. 13 year-old Sophie and her best friend Mari were messing around with her phone camera and taking sexy pictures of themselves. They were emailing and texting them back and forth to each other. When their friend Asha came over, they showed her what they'd been doing.

Later, Ella and Asha were with their boyfriends and Ella told them what she and Sophie had been doing earlier that day. The boys got Asha to ask Sophie to send her a sext and Sophie, not knowing what was going on, did! Asha showed it off and that seemed to be the end of the story.

The next day, Asha met her boyfriend for breakfast and he started fooling around with her phone. Guess what? He forwarded himself the sext of Ella and then proceeded to forward it to a bunch of his guy friends.

Ella found out what happened when one of her Facebook friends, a very, very nice boy, posted "You shouldn't send pictures like that of yourself." Ella was mortified and immediately shut down her Facebook account, under the advice of a savvy older friend.

Ella spent nearly a week feeling embarrassed, ashamed and completely stupid for thinking she could sext and get away with it. She finally told her parents and then, not surprisingly, everyone involved got in trouble.

As a teen it's really easy to get caught up in the moment and then make really stupid decision because your brain isn't quite up to thinking things through all the way. Figure out a way to stop before you do something - you might try counting 25 or 50 or 100. If you are by yourself, do a quick pro and con list, get up and walk away from the computer or the phone.

Wait it out.

If you are with friends, say "maybe" say you need to pee to buy some time, set up a code with a friend beforehand that means "I'm not into this," or do something that buys you some thinking time.

It can be really super hard to resist doing something on impulse, I don't want you thinking it's easy, because it's really not. Practice your impulse resistance skills on something easy - like whether to eat three bowls of cereal instead of four, or limiting yourself to a certain amount of screen time and no more.

Your Crazy Parents

If you haven't already noticed, this business of being a teenager is probably making your parents crazy. This is a hard time for them, too—you want more independence, and they know how wild the world is, so they are afraid to let you go. Add in some crazy "brain development" behavior on your part and your parents are going to be even more whacked out by the whole thing.

Many parents don't know about this brain development stuff, so you might lovingly fill them in. If they know that (sometimes) you aren't doing the things they find annoying on purpose, they may calm down a little or at least treat you differently.

In theory, their brains are fully developed, so they should be able to think things through with much more ease than you can in certain circumstances. Even adults forget to do this and your parents might react without thinking, just like you. If you are having a fight with your mom or dad (or anyone else, really), and realize how upset and angry you all are, tell them you need to take a break from the conversation. Then go somewhere, like your room or the bathroom, and hang out until you calm down.

It's kind of a bummer that you should be the one taking care of the relationship, but someone needs to, and things will go much, much better in the long run if you show this moment of maturity. They will remember it.

Stuff to Think About!

What have you noticed about the effects of your changing brain?

Has your relationship with your parents changed since you started puberty? What do you think about this?

How have you been affected by sexting? Your friends? What will you do if (when, really) you receive a sext?

Think about some situations when you could have said "maybe" and been happier with your choice. How can you remember to use the maybe trick next time?

CHAPTER FOUR

Romantic Love Versus Family Love: What's the difference?

Love is very confusing—there is little doubt about this! There are many different kinds of love, and it's helpful to have some understanding of these different types. You have probably already experienced family and friend love. This type of love is usually unconditional—you love the person even though they make you nuts, are sometimes mean, and occasionally make bad decisions. This kind of love isn't sexual.

You will also come to know romantic love—the wonderful, passionate, and sexual feelings of love you will have for your boyfriend, girlfriend, someday husband, wife, or life partner. In long-term relationships, love becomes more of a combination of romantic love and family love, but ideally there are still strong feelings of romantic love.

Love Really Shouldn't Hurt!

In a healthy relationship of any type—romantic, family, or friendship— love should not hurt. (We'll talk more about this in chapters 9 and 10.) If you are experiencing violence or abuse of any kind—physical, verbal, or sexual—in any of your relationships, you need help and support. The person who is abusing you needs help as well, but this isn't your responsibility. Your responsibility is to yourself. As hard as it may be to admit, it is very important you tell someone you trust.

The abuse is not your fault. Ever. No matter what the abusive person in your life says or does, it is never your fault. You may need to ask for help more than one time, it's hard, but keep asking until someone listens to you. School counselors are a great resource and source of support.

If you are abusing someone, and you know if you are, get help. Tell someone like a teacher, trusted adult, parent, or a friend. There are many places you can go to get help and support so you too can start the path to recovery (see the Resources section at the end of the book).

Family and Friend Love

Even though your parents and family may be driving you completely crazy and your family situation may not be perfect, the love you feel for them should be a positive experience. The love you feel for your friends is usually very similar to the love you may feel for your family.

You may be in a family with many problems—divorce, alcoholism, money troubles, or abuse. Your experience of "family love" may not fit the ideal. If you are in this kind of family, finding someone to talk to can help.

Ideal family and friendship love can be:

- Unconditional—you are loved no matter what you do or say

- Non-judgmental

- Warm

- Long-lasting

- Steady

- Comfortable

- Encouraging

You may not be feeling tons of love and warm, fuzzy feelings for your family these days. This is part of separating from your parents so you can learn how to be an independent adult. Nevertheless, take a minute and think about how you experience love in your family.

Thinking about how you experience love in your family and with your friends can help you be clearer about romantic love. Understanding the difference will provide some help when you are starting on—or are in the middle of—a romance. Once passion, attraction, and desire hit the scene, love can get truly mystifying.

Romantic Love

Romantic love is different from family love and is one of the most exhilarating, bewildering, fun, exciting, life-changing things ever. As romantic relationships age, the love you feel for your partner will develop elements of family and friendship love. All good romances definitely feel like good friendships, too.

Romantic love is usually:

- Passionate

- Sexual

- Conditional

- Unplanned

- Fleeting

- Unpredictable

- Chemical/hormonal

The biggest difference between family love and romantic love is that it's passionate and sexual. The next biggest difference between the two is that romantic love is conditional. This means if your romantic partner does something you don't agree with or hurts your feelings, your feeling of love for them can fade away. With family love, if your feelings are hurt or something happens that you don't agree with, chances are your feelings of love for your parent or sibling remain.

Romantic love is fleeting—it can vanish in a nanosecond. Family love endures good times and bad times. Romantic love is unplanned and unpredictable. Perhaps you suddenly have a crush on your best friend's boyfriend or girlfriend. You didn't plan this—it just happened. Surprise! You're in love. On the other hand, we are born into our families and can't help but love them in a way that is hard to shake.

Romantic love has a ton to do with chemicals and hormones in your body. Have you ever noticed how someone you are romantically interested in smells really good to you? This is an example of the chemical and hormonal ingredient of romantic love. These hormones and chemicals are all about sex. Our bodies want us to find people to reproduce with that complement our genes. You can intellectualize all you want, but if you just aren't attracted to someone in a physical way, there really isn't any way to force attraction to happen.

Sexual desire can fool you into thinking you are in love with someone. That strong surge of desire you feel when you see someone you are attracted to can feel a lot like romantic love. It's exhilarating, exciting, overwhelming, and generally feels darned good. This desire can be a major distraction when you are dating someone because those feelings can cloud your judgment about your true feelings for that person.

It is very difficult to tell the difference between lust and love, especially in the heat of the moment. So, if you find yourself in a relationship that is proceeding physically, but when you are away from that person you aren't so sure about them, you might want to reconsider the relationship.

What's the Difference?

As you may have noticed, guys and girls are wired a bit differently when it comes to sex and love. Here's a little info to show you some of the differences. Remember, these differences don't apply to everyone. Understanding where the other person may be coming from is helpful when you are thinking about your relationships.

Guys and Sexuality

The sex hormone, testosterone, is 20 percent higher in teen guys than in teen girls. It is thought that this makes guys more interested in sex for the sake of sex than girls are.

Guys are at the height of their sex drive in their teens.

Guys are more likely to think about sex and being physical with someone rather than love and intimacy in the relationship.

Sometimes guys will tell someone they "love" them because they think it's the right thing to say at a certain point in the relationship or it will get the other person to make out or have sex with them.

Many guys see having sex as an act of romance, while most women do not.

Teen guys can act confident and savvy when it comes to sex, but in reality they are often confused and conflicted about it.

Lots of guys feel guilty about having sex because they manipulated their partner into it, wish they had waited, or weren't that into their partner in the first place.

Girls and Sexuality

Girls have just as strong feelings of sexual desire as guys. They are socialized to pretend they don't.

Girls don't hit their sexual peak until their thirties, so sometimes teen girls don't feel the strong need for sex that teen guys do.

Most teen girls believe sex is an expression of love and prefer signs of affection to sex.

Attraction is definitely part of the game for teen girls and women, but often the goal isn't to have sex but to be emotionally close to them—which can then lead to sexual intimacy.

Teen girls are more likely to think about and focus on feelings of love and intimacy in a relationship rather than sex and being physical.

Often, teen girls feel bad about their bodies and will choose to have sex because they feel insecure about themselves.

Many teen girls enjoy their sexual experiences with the right partner, protection, and a clear understanding of the relationship.

Teen girls can see sex as an indicator of a deep commitment to a relationship and are often disappointed to discover their partners don't share the same level of commitment.

Lots of teen girls feel guilty about having sex because they manipulated their partner into it, wish they had waited, or weren't that into their partner in the first place.

41

What's the Benefit of Friends With Benefits and Hooking Up?

"Friends with benefits" and hooking up sounds like it would be easy and totally doable, but in reality is pretty much impossible to pull off without someone getting hurt. The idea is that you agree to have sex (or fool around) with someone "as friends" but without having any romantic relationship—you aren't dating; you're just having sex. So, here's the deal: it is really hard to have sex with someone and remain friends.

Take Crystal and Isaac, for example. Crystal really liked her friend Isaac; they were just friends, but she thought he was cute and funny and had a super-secret crush on him. One night, they'd been at a party, and one thing led to another and they ended up having sex. They talked about it afterwards—it "just happened" —and decided that it was fun and they should just have sex with each other, but not a relationship. No strings, just fun, no worries. Right? Ha!

Crystal went along with this because she thought she'd be able to sway him over to a real relationship. Isaac was happy because he liked her, liked sex, and knew he was going away to college at the end of the summer so it would all be super casual. Can you see the recipe for disaster here?

Needless to say, Crystal tried to make their relationship more like a dating relationship by calling and texting and making plans. Isaac was really only interested in hanging out as friends and doing "the deed." He didn't want a girlfriend. He thought he'd made this clear, but Crystal had her own agenda. Long story short? She ended up with her heart broken because he didn't want a relationship and their friendship was ruined, too.

Sex complicates relationships in many ways, the least of which is the possibility of getting pregnant or getting an STI.

If you are having sex with someone, pregnancy can be a possibility, so it's smart to consider whether you are ready to become a parent and whether this person is someone you want to have a relationship with for the rest of your life. This may not necessarily be a romantic relationship, but it very well may be a co-parenting relationship!

Are you having romantic or sexual thoughts about a friend? You could be heading into some feelings of romantic love. Many romances begin as friendships, and getting to know someone as a friend helps to establish trust. It can be a really good thing to be friends before the romance happens.

Is a friend having romantic thoughts about you? If you already know that you don't feel the same way, don't make the mistake of dating them anyway. It's not fair to lead them on. If you aren't sure, spend more time together as friends, get to know each other better, and maybe your feelings will change.

It is very easy to take advantage of someone if you are in this position and "friends with benefits" often starts here. You figure, "They're willing. I've been clear that this is nothing but sex and we're not dating. It's all good."

The other person thinks they can handle it and that through their amazing skills in bed, they'll hook you in and make you fall in love. Most likely, this isn't going to work out to anyone's advantage. Just think for a moment about the people you know who have been in this situation. Ultimately, it can be messy and not as much fun as you thought.

Being in Love

Adults sometimes think that teens can't possibly be "in love." I'm not sure why they think this, because a significant number of them were in love when they were teens. One of the reasons for this has to do with looking back on their lives and "knowing what they know now." They think their "grown-up" love is more "real" than their teenage love ever was. Ask your parents if they were "in love" as teenagers and then ask them if their feelings were real.

They may think their grow-up love is more "real" because their relationships are more "mature" and may be longer lasting. The truth is, people fall in love over and over again, all throughout their lives, and each time feels real and true. Adults wouldn't get married and divorced at the rate they do if love wasn't part of the program. Love is love, no matter how old you are. If you are in love with your boyfriend or girlfriend, you are truly in love. It's pretty simple.

Understanding the difference between family, friendship, and romantic love will help you understand your feelings in your romantic relationships. Knowing if you are in love is one of the most challenging things about being in a relationship. Being able to sort out your feelings of friendship from your romantic feelings is a good place to start.

Stuff to Think About!

How do your parents or family show you they love you?

How do you show your parents or family that you love them?

How do you know your friends love you?

How do you know if you should date a friend?

How do you show your friends you love them?

What's important to you about this way of looking at love?

Think about someone you have a crush on. Do you think they are truly boy- or girlfriend material? Why or why not?

If you know someone has a crush on you, how can you show

them you are interested in dating? In not dating?

What has changed about how you think about love and sex after reading this chapter?

CHAPTER FIVE

Are You Normal? Yeah, Most Likely

The number one concern of every teenager is this: "Am I normal?" The answer is "Most likely, yes!" When you're a teen there is so much change going on emotionally, mentally, physically, and socially it's really hard to know what's normal.

One minute you're happy, the next depressed. You might be impulsive and make crazy decisions that afterward leave you wondering, "What the heck was I thinking?!" This is standard stuff for teenagers and nearly everyone you know has experienced some of these feelings in varying degrees.

Your teen years are a time of learning about and developing your own morals, values, and beliefs that are separate from your parents' and friends'. You may be on the same page about some things and be at complete odds about others. "Normal" is a word that is full of judgment as it implies that something is wrong with you if you don't have behaviors (or beliefs) that are typical or expected by others around you.

When it comes to sexuality there are some behaviors that are common in your age group, which means lots of teens have reported having these experiences. There are also behaviors that are uncommon, and if you are engaging in these, or know someone who is, it might be time to get some help. If you are not sure, you can easily find out by anonymously contacting one of the resources listed at the end of the book.

Here are some common teenage sexual behaviors[1]:

Asking questions and wondering about decision-making, social relationships, and sexual customs.

Masturbating in private.

Experimenting with teens of the same age (and sometimes the same sex), including open-mouthed kissing, fondling and body rubbing, oral/genital contact and sexual intercourse.

Spying on people for sexual stimulation (voyeurism).

Looking at pornography.

Nearly half of high-school students have sex[2].

Uncommon sexual behaviors in teens[3]:

Masturbating in public.

Sexual interest in much younger children.

I'm a big fan of understanding what is considered "normal" which is why I included this list. If you are doing something that isn't on this list or that you are worried about, contact one of the resources at the end of the book. Chances are good you will discover there is nothing wrong with you, and if you do need help, there are plenty of folks who will help you get it.

Who Do You Like?

Another aspect of sexuality has to do with attraction—your sexual orientation. Who turns you on? Guys? Girls? Both? You may be relieved to find out that sexual attraction is on a continuum. This means that it can vary from being completely heterosexual (only attracted to the opposite sex) to being completely homosexual (only attracted to the same sex). People can also be attracted to the same sex some of the time and the opposite sex some of the time.

The people you are emotionally, romantically, or sexually attracted to is primarily about how you are wired—it is an instinctive, naturally occurring part of who you are and it isn't something that can be controlled, fundamentally changed, or "unlearned."[4]

Just for clarity's sake, heterosexual or straight means you are sexually and romantically attracted to people of the opposite sex. Homosexual or gay/lesbian means you are sexually and romantically attracted to people of the same sex. Bisexual or bi means you are sexually and romantically attracted to people of both sexes.

Here's more detailed information about sexual orientation.[5] You may be:

- Completely heterosexual—never attracted to the same sex and don't have sex with people of the same sex

- Primarily heterosexual—rarely attracted to the same sex and rarely have sex with people of the same sex

- Mostly heterosexual—sometimes attracted to the same sex and sometimes have sex with people of the same sex

- Bisexual—Equally heterosexual and homosexual

- Mostly homosexual—sometimes attracted to the opposite sex and sometimes have sex with people of the opposite sex

- Primarily homosexual—rarely attracted to the opposite sex and rarely have sex with people of the opposite sex

- Completely homosexual—never attracted to the opposite sex and never have sex with people of the opposite sex

- Asexual or non-sexual—no sexual feelings for anyone

All of these orientations are considered "normal." Just like heterosexuals, nearly every gay or lesbian person will tell you they were born that way. There is more and more evidence to show that this is true. If you are heterosexual and you can't imagine being gay or lesbian and think it is wrong, (or maybe your family or religion says it is) I would encourage you to remember that a person's sexual orientation is a personal and private thing. Everyone deserves respect, even if you don't agree with him or her.

Where you find yourself on this scale may change throughout your lifetime, especially if you find yourself somewhere in the middle. This too, is normal.

A Word About Sex, Gender and Transgender

Transgender is probably something you've heard about, but don't quite understand. I'm going to attempt to explain it to you—it can be confusing and this is the world's simplest explanation of something super complicated. Please hang in there with me.

A person's biological sex is whether they are born physically female or male. When most people are born, it's very clear they are male or female. (Sometimes, it's not so clear, physically, but that's a story for another day). To keep this simple, think about biological sex as male or female.

Gender is two things working together and the words we use to describe gender are girl/woman and man/boy. The first thing is gender identity—how a person feels on the inside and how they think about themselves as a male or female person. The second is gender expression—how a person shows up in the world. This is how they dress, act, behave, etc. Usually a person's gender and their biological sex are For example, I am female and I feel like a woman on the inside and I dress and behave (most of the time) like other women do. This is called being "cisgender."

Sometimes, a person's gender doesn't match their sex and this is called transgender. I believe this is a just another normal way of being. Kind of like being gay, it can be really hard for the person who is transgender because it's super confusing and misunderstood. The good news is there is a lot of help for transgender people these days. If you are wondering about your gender check out the Resources section for more info.

Lust or Sexual Desire

Another thing that varies from person to person is their level of desire. Just like sexual orientation, there is a continuum of desire. Some people are more sexual (feel more sexual feelings, and are more interested in sex and sexual activity) than others. Once again, this is a personal and fundamental part of who you are.

There are times in your life when you may feel more sexual (for a lot of you that's right now!) and times when you will feel less sexual. Again, this ebb and flow is a natural part of being human. The key is to respect your partner's level of desire especially if they are less sexual than you. If you need a way to deal with your sexual desire see page 79.

You may wonder, "How much is too much thinking about sex?" As a teen you may be thinking about sex all the time. This isn't entirely your fault—all those hormones coursing through your veins have something to do with this. Your body is at its peak for reproduction so your biology works hard to get you to make some babies—or at least practice. And, we live in a sexually saturated culture, so you are bombarded with stimulating images all the time.

As a rule of thumb (and this really applies to just about any aspect of your life) if you are thinking about someone to the point that it distracts you from your ability to get through your day, do your homework, hang with your friends, do sports, or the things you love, then you may have a problem. If you feel weird, yucky, sad, scared, or gross when you think about sex or a person, it might be time to seek some help. Ultimately, this sex and relationship stuff should feel really, really great—physically and emotionally.

A Rant About . . . Wanking
(That's Masturbation if You're in Britain)!

There are many ways to handle your feelings of sexual desire— masturbation (touching your penis or clitoris for pleasure) being one of the safest and most convenient. Seriously, it works every time and there isn't anyone else involved so you don't have worry about hurt feelings or complex relationship issues. It is perfectly normal to masturbate and perfectly nor-mal not to masturbate, it's a personal choice.

Guys—if you are wondering what's too much, it most likely isn't too much unless you are doing it every single chance you get, morning, noon and night, in public or you are physically hurt- ing yourself. Then you might have a problem.

Girls—this is a life skill, so get to know your body because it's a truly magical thing. In the long run, the more familiar you are with your body—your likes and dislikes—the better your sex life will be. It's smart for you to know how your body works and what works for you sexually, so you don't get confused and think your someday sex partner is wholly responsible for those great sexual feelings.

Pornography And You (or Amy Rants About Porn)

At this point in your life, you've probably seen some kind of pornography either on the Internet or in magazines. Don't worry, it's completely normal to be curious about, or interested in, pornography because it can be a turn on, and it feels good to be excited.

Porn is one of those things people have very strong feelings about, both pro and con. These days it is incredibly easy to view pornography since it is just a click away. It's also amazingly easy to find yourself at a porn site that is really over the top—violent, graphic, involving children or teens, and just downright creepy.

Some people think that it's healthy for teens to view porn. They think it's an outlet for sexual desire, it's a solo activity, there's no risk of infection or pregnancy, and it's mostly harmless. I think at its core, porn is degrading to women and girls and gives people a false idea about sex, sexuality, bodies and its role in relationships.

Porn turns women into objects used for one thing only—sex. This is called "objectification" and when someone is objectified it makes it much easier to deny their humanness, their uniqueness, and their personhood. Objectification can lead to all sorts of cruddy stuff, like violence, rape, low self-esteem, eating disorders and unrealistic expectations.[6]

One interesting thing about pornography is that teens are getting a serious amount of information about sex by watching it. A very cool survey of guys shows that they learn as much about sex from porn as they do from their parents and other trustworthier sources.[7] Honestly, porn is one of the worst places to learn about sex and relationships because it's not real!

Here are some things to keep in mind about pornography:

It is the rare person whose body looks like that! Porn gives the viewer a warped idea of women's (and men's) bodies.

Viewing porn can be overwhelming to your developing heart

and mind because you really aren't prepared or ready to fully understand the images and what they mean. It's overload.

It sets up unrealistic expectations of sex. Frankly, the vast majority of sexual experiences are nothing like what you'd see in pornography. Check out MakeLoveNotPorn.com for a comparison between what porn teaches and reality.

It makes sex an emotionless experience, which can make it hard to relate to real live people when the time comes.

If you've trained yourself to be stimulated by something that isn't based in reality, it can make it difficult to give and receive sexual pleasure from another person.

Would you want your sister or brother, cousin, friend, mother, or grandmother involved in something like this? If you feel like barfing at the thought of this, think about it the next time you go online to visit a porn site.

Maybe you're thinking, "I look at porn and I'm just fine!" If this is the case, I'd ask you to look a little deeper into this belief. If you find yourself obsessively looking at porn or feel that it's the only way you can "get off," you may have a problem. This can happen to both guys and girls. There are some resources at the end of the book if you think you might need help.

There is a wide range of what is considered "normal" sexual behavior. There are many different ways to be sexual, have relationships, or to learn about sexuality. If you still feel like you aren't "normal" in some way after reading this chapter, please find someone to talk to about your feelings. There is help available for just about every problem out there, you just need to ask for it. See the resources section for some ideas of places to get help.

Stuff to Think About!

What do you think about what's considered "normal" sexual behavior for teens?

Imagine you live in a world where it is normal for everyone to be dating and/or marrying someone of the same sex. How would you feel? If you are heterosexual, what kind of insight does this give you into being gay, lesbian, or bisexual?

What do you think about masturbation? Do you agree that it's a healthy thing to do?

Does viewing porn go with your values? Why or why not?

CHAPTER SIX

Wanna Go to the Movies? A Fake First Date

One thing you can do to become a super dater is to create a list of "rules" for dating you. These "rules" are things that are important to you regarding how you want to be treated and what's important to you in a partner. When you are clear about this it makes it much easier to know if you should be dating someone. If they break a rule you'll know the relationship is in trouble and can make a decision about whether you want it to continue.

To get prepared to develop your set of rules for dating, let's walk through a first date situation. To make this process easier, I've simplified things a bit, but I hope you'll get some good stuff out of this by the time you finish this chapter.

You'll look at what to do if you get asked out and don't want to date the person, do want to date the person or are not sure. You'll read about how to ask someone out, who pays, what to wear, general dating tips, whether to get physical and how to end a date well.

Even though you will probably do a whole bunch of talking via text you still need plan out what you'll say and how you'll say it. Texts can last forever, get sent around, and aren't really private. Do you want everyone to know how you handled a sticky dating situation, especially if you didn't do it well? Didn't think so.

You'll be asked to think about some scripts (what you want to say before you say it), which might seem silly and awkward at first, but they are really helpful and no one will know they are scripts—you'll just seem like you've got it together! At the end of this "first date," you'll work on creating your rules for dating you.

You Ask Someone Out!

You've finally decided to ask out that guy or girl you've had a crush on since first grade. This can be nerve wracking! Having a script will make the experience much easier.

You could say "Hey! I was wondering if you'd like to go out with me next Friday night. We could go to the movies. Is there something you've been wanting to see?"

Be specific about what you want to do—meet at a party, go to the mall, go out for dinner, go to the movies, whatever. You should be prepared for both acceptance and rejection, so take a deep, cleansing breath and dive in.

If they say "no thanks" you will probably feel a little embarrassed, crushed (maybe that's why they call it a crush), and maybe even sad. How you respond is very important because they may change their mind—maybe not, but it's best to be gracious.

You can say something like "Okay. That's cool. See you later." And then move on!

Someone Just Asked You Out!

Someone has asked you out. Maybe you're interested, maybe you're not, and maybe you're not sure. Your responsibility, no matter what, is to be polite and friendly at all times. Think about how hard it is to get up the courage to ask someone out. First, consider how you feel, what your gut reaction is to this person asking you out.

What To Do if You Don't Want to Date Them!

You've just been asked out by:

That weird guy or girl in your math class.

That guy or girl you met at the mall and stupidly gave your phone number.

Your cousin's best friend who gives you the total creeps or is totally annoying.

You have zero interest in going out with this person because you don't like them, are already involved with someone, or any other good reason you may have, and need to say "no thanks." First of all—and this is really important—put yourself in their shoes! Think about how vulnerable you would feel in this moment.

Here's an example of what NOT to do:

Eric had a huge crush on this moderately popular girl named Tami. He wasn't very popular, but they talked all the time in math class and he helped her out a lot. He got up the nerve to ask her out and made the mistake of doing it within hearing of her group of friends.

She said "No way!" laughed, and flounced away, back to her giggling group of friends. Ouch. He felt terrible: embarrassed, disrespected, and hurt. He thought they were at least friends and didn't expect her to be so mean.

How would you want to be treated if you had put yourself out there like this? Laughed at? Ignored? Probably not. So be as nice as you can when you say "no."

You could say, "How nice/sweet of you to ask me out, but I'm really interested in just being friends with you. Thanks though." If you can, get out of there as soon as possible so you don't have to hang out and be uncomfortable.

You can always say "maybe" and then get back to them later with a "no." It's kinder to say "no" right away because no one likes to be left hanging. If you say "maybe" be sure to get back to them within a couple of hours.

Whatever you do, don't go out on "mercy dates," because you feel sorry for the person. They set up false hopes. If you go out with someone because you're leveraged into a double date, make it clear from the beginning you aren't interested in them romantically. And for goodness sake, don't fool around with someone if you aren't all that interested in them.

What to Do If You Want to Date Them!

You've just been asked out by:

- Your long-time crush.

- That guy or girl who always talks to you in French class.

- A girl or guy you met at a basketball game from another school whom you've been texting.

You say "yes!" and decide to go out on Friday night.

Let's assume you are allowed to go on this date (we'll ditch the conservative parent rules for the sake of this exercise).

The plan is to have something to eat and go to a movie. First of all, communicate with your family and tell your parents:

- Who you're going out with – ideally the person will meet your parents.

- Where you're going and who else is going to be there.

58

- How you'll get there and get home.

- When you'll be home.

When you let your parents know the plan this shows you are mature and think things through. Your parents will worry less and will feel more confident about your ability to handle yourself appropriately, which is a good thing.

Who's Going to Pay?

If you can, get this out of the way early, before you even go on the date. Often it's assumed that the person who did the asking out also pays for everything. It's also often assumed that if the guy did the asking out, he pays. If you've been asked on a date, it's safest to assume everything will be split. This way, if you need to pay for yourself, you'll be ready for it.

This can also be a little safety net if, after the first ten minutes, you know you never want to see this person again. Splitting the bill gives you some control over the situation. Then you can announce you feel like barfing, call your mom, and get the heck out of there.

It may be a little awkward to talk about who's going to pay, but it's better to be up front about it and avoid any surprises. You can also wait until you're faced with a bill and then ask, "Do you want to split it?" This is the polite thing to do.

If you did the asking out, be prepared to pay for everything. It's bad form for the person who did the asking out to want to split the bill without arranging with the other person in advance that the expenses on the date would be shared.

For example, you need to make it clear before you are on the date that you can afford to pay for the movie tickets, but will need to split dinner. This gives your date the opportunity to say, "Let's skip dinner and just do the movie." You should say

59

this if you can't afford dinner. This is one time when texting is a really great way to communicate.

What Are You Going to Wear?

Our clothes send a message to people about who we are, and people can be very judgmental about clothes and appearance. Keep this question in mind when you are figuring out what to wear—"What decisions or judgments could my date possibly make about me based on what I'm wearing?" Think about everything and decide if that's what you want someone thinking about you.

What might your date think if you showed up wearing something:

- Sloppy, old, or dirty.

- Short, revealing, or sexy.

- Plain, boring, and simple.

- Super casual like yoga pants or sweats.

- Really, really expensive.

- Clearly second hand.

- Super funky or really unique and individual.

- Just like everyone else.

You totally need to be you and I know you have your own particular style. Be true to your style—don't try to be someone you aren't—but keep in mind that people make snap decisions based on appearance.

You're Out on the Date!

You've connected and are hanging out before the movie, walking around, trying to figure out where to eat. Relax and ask them questions about themselves. Your date will feel more comfortable if you seem interested in them and it will give you something to do!

A Few Dating Tips!

Be on time and if you are running late, let them know as soon as possible.

Let your date know when you are expected to be home, find out when they are expected to be home and reconfirm your plans.

Don't answer your phone unless it's your parents, the people you're meeting with, or some other appropriate person for you to be talking to at this time. Your best friend doesn't count.

No texting. It's rude! Even if your date is doing it, you don't need to be rude, too.

Compliment them. A lot.

Ask them questions about themselves, school, family, sports, movies they've seen, books they've read, favorite games, music, web sites, elementary school, travels, etc.

If you have been talking a blue streak, shut up, and let them get a word in edgewise.

Don't be weird about food (girls, this means you). Eat something. If you are a "picky eater" and someone has asked you to dinner, don't make a big deal out of it and find something, anything, to eat. It's a real bummer to be out to dinner with someone who won't eat.

61

Don't talk about how fat, ugly, or stupid you are. This makes it seem like you are fishing for compliments and is boring. You can talk to your best friend about this stuff.

Don't pretend to like something if you don't really like it. The truth will eventually come out, especially if this date turns out to be the first of many.

If your date steals something, suggests you do drugs, drink alcohol, wants to leave the mall, "accidentally" meets his or her group of friends, or otherwise does something illegal or that just ticks you off or freaks you out, make up an excuse to get out of the situation and leave (see chapter 7).

If your date is pressuring you to have sex or make out or do anything physical that you aren't comfortable with, find a way to get out of the situation and head on home (see chapter 7).

If there is no "spark" (and you'll know if there is one) don't pretend there is one just to get free food, to fool around, have sex, or get oral sex. This is unfair and disrespectful—to both of you.

Guys, just because she decided to wear something sexy do not assume she wants to have sex.

If your date seems distracted, like they keep answering their phone, texting, and otherwise ignoring you, consider ending the date early.

If you think your date is the most boring human being on the planet you are obligated to suffer through the date. This stinks, but you'll feel better about yourself than if you bail on them mid-date. You can easily live through an hour of food and two hours of a movie—it's not the end of the world. You don't need to go out with them again.

Get home on time.

Should We Hold Hands or More?

Perhaps you want to hold your date's hand, kiss them, or put your arm around their shoulder. Sometimes the opportunity presents itself and it is very clear that it's okay to do this. Most of the time you probably won't be so sure if it's okay.

Try to read body signals. If she turns her head away from you when you are going in for a kiss, quickly change direction and the subject. If he cringes, winces, or lets go of your hand as soon as he possibly can, he's probably not into holding your hand.

Pay attention to your date's reactions and you will know if you have overstepped a boundary. Then, respect their boundaries and don't try to force them to do something they don't want to do or aren't ready to do. Go slowly and you will figure it out. This doesn't seem like much help, but this is something you need to get a feel for by observation and through experience.

You're at the movie and suddenly there's an arm around your shoulders, a hand in your crotch, or something else going on that makes you uncomfortable.

Here are some very clever things you can say nicely—or not— and do to get them to back off:

Pick their hand up put it back in their lap, and whisper, "I think this is yours."

Arm over your shoulder crushing you? Lean forward like you are tying your shoe, and when you sit back up, their arm should be back where it belongs. If it's not, lean over and say, "I'm sorry! Your arm weighs a ton!" If you must, help them put it back where it belongs.

Announce you need to go to the bathroom and will be right

back. Come back, if you don't feel threatened. Or, depending on what's been going on, leave. Send them a text and tell them you decided to go home (after you leave) and apologize. You can explain later if you need to.

It is always okay to bail out on a date if you feel threatened, frightened or really uncomfortable. You need to let your date know you are leaving. You can always ask an adult (yes, a stranger!) to help you if you are very upset or scared. There is a 99.99% chance that adult will help you.

The Date Is Over!

You made it through, and now it's time to say goodnight. You need to decide for yourself—one of "your" rules—just how you end a first date. Whether there is any kissing, hugging, or any other physical contact, will depend on how the date went, how you feel about the person (and how they feel about you), and if you want to go out with each other again. A hug is certainly the safest, neutral, thanks-I-had-fun-perhaps-we-can-do-this-again thing to do.

What will be your standard, fall back, thanks-for-the-nice-time good-bye? You won't always stick to this, but it's good to have a guideline, which may save your butt (and someone else's ego).

You could say "Oh! I don't like to kiss anyone on the first date—it's just a funny rule I have—nothing personal!" Of course, if they push it, don't respect your boundaries, or whine and complain, you can consider this a "red flag" to not go out with them again. It's all about respect, right?

If you're not interested in seeing them again, you don't need to tell them at this very moment, unless it's abundantly clear and you want to get it over with. It's fine to call them or send them a text later and let them down gently.

Post-date Assessment

How'd it go? Did you have fun? Were they respectful of you? Did they seem interested in you? Did anything seem weird, off, or make you uncomfortable? Do you want to go out with them again? Do you have things in common?

Only you know if you had a good time with this person and feel comfortable around them. If you are not sure, or are have one of those strange feelings about the person you can't quite name (something just feels off), think long and hard about whether you want to see them again.

Always—unless they were truly awful—call, e-mail, or send a text thanking them for the date. This is the respectful thing to do. If they ask you out again and you don't want to see them, let them down nicely. Don't be mean. Thank them and just be neutral and nice.

You could say "I had a nice time with you, but I think I'd rather be just friends. Thanks for the dinner and movie. See you later." You don't have to explain, just make it short and kind.

What if they never call or text you again and you thought you both had a good time? Ouch. This is one of the stinky parts of dating: rejection. It's no fun, it hurts, and can be confusing. It can be especially confusing if you fooled around or had sex on your date.

Here's a wee tale of woe from a girl named Tara. She met a guy at a Halloween party and ended up fooling around with him a little. She gave him her phone number and about a week later he called her and asked if she could come over to his house. Tara was super flattered and excited—he was really cute and nice and older—so she zipped over to his house.

65

When she got there, his parents weren't home and after he got her something to drink, they immediately started making out. One thing led to another and she ended up giving him oral sex, even though she really didn't want to. She went home feeling pretty yucky, and never heard from him again. She called him a couple of times, but he never called back. Rejection central.

If you called or texted three times and still haven't gotten a response: stop trying to contact them. They clearly aren't interested in the fabulousness that is you, and you don't want to get a reputation of being a stalker. No matter what they said, or what you did, this person obviously just isn't that into you. There are a bazillion people in the world and there certainly is at least one for you—just not this one.

You're Ready for Another Date!

You had fun, they had fun, you've texted and talked, and it seems like all systems are "go." Ask them out again and you are off and running. Super fun!

Stuff to Think About!

Think about how you react to the clothing people wear. When have you made a decision about someone and been wrong?

What dating mistakes have you made in the past? What could you have done differently? Do you owe anyone an apology?

What other dating tips have people given you?

Have your parents talked to you about their rules for dating?

What is your "rule" for ending a date—a hug, a kiss, a hand-shake?

CHAPTER SEVEN

Slow It Down or Speed It Up?
Bumps in the Dating Road

There are some situations you need to be prepared to deal with in your dating life, such as how to escape a bad date, pressure, deal breakers, trusting your intuition, dating friends, and dating and sex.

Escape Plan 101

You may find yourself in a situation on a date, or even when you are out with friends, that is uncomfortable, scary, or just seems like a bad idea and you need to get out of it. It's smart to have some kind of escape plan so you can get away without looking stupid.

It's best to have your parents or another trustworthy adult in on it, so you may need to have a chat with them about your escape plan. This is probably something they haven't thought of providing for you, so you get to look super responsible by proposing one.

Fifteen-year-old Josh has the following planned with his parents: they have a secret code so he can get rescued from sticky situations without his friends knowing what's going on.

He calls his parents because he has to "check in or they'll kill him." Then, when he's on the phone with them and he asks, "Is that the dog barking in the back ground?" they know something is up and he needs rescuing. They come and get him immediately. This is a great tip for dates-gone-bad or any other time!

Develop your own secret code and plan with your parents (and keep it to yourself so you don't lose face). It could save you a lot of trouble.

List of "Get Me Outta Here!" Situations

Pick the top three situations that will send you running for the hills:

- Your date or friends are ignoring you.

- Your date or friends are being mean to you or someone else.

- A major change of plans has been proposed.

- Your date or friends want to go somewhere with a group of older people.

- Your date or friends want to go somewhere with a group of teens you just met.

- People you are with are kissing and getting together and you don't want to.

- People you are with are kissing and getting together and you don't have anyone to kiss or get together with.

- Your date is pressuring you to have sex or go farther than you are comfortable.

- People are drinking/doing drugs.

- Your ride or date has been drinking/doing drugs.

- Your date has done or said something that makes you feel really uncomfortable.

- People are making plans to do something illegal— graffiti, steal something, buy drugs, etc.

Even though you've picked out the three scenarios you find most uncomfortable, nothing compares to real life. Right now, it's easy to think, "I can get out of these situations. No problem!" In reality, it's really, really hard – and you may know that because of your own experinece. However, thinking these through now and being even a little bit prepared goes a long way towards being brave later.

When you have a general "rescue plan" in place, it will make it significantly easier to get out of uncomfortable or dangerous situations. Decide whom you will call or text if you need help and be sure to have a back up person, just in case. Talk to these people and let them know you have chosen them to come to your rescue if you need them.

Deal Breakers: When It Might Be Time to Dump Your Date

A "deal breaker" is something—a behavior, comment, or value—you absolutely cannot tolerate and violates your trust, faith, or good opinion of someone. The "deal" is basically an unspoken agreement between you and the other person that you will treat each other with respect and kindness.

Nobody ever talks about this deal, it's usually just understood and assumed. If someone breaks the "deal" you have with them about what it takes to be lucky enough to date you, it means you won't date them again. As an example, violence of any kind towards you or someone one else should be high on your list of deal breakers.

Take a look at the following list. Which are your top five deal breakers? This will help you sort out your rules.

- Violence of any kind toward anyone

- Verbal and emotional abuse

- Drinking or drug use

- They ignore you

- Excessive texting or phone calling

- Obsessive social media us or gaming

- Unsafe driving

- Disrespect of you, your beliefs, your family, or friends

- A creepy, uncomfortable, icky feeling about the person

- Unwanted sexual contact of any kind

- They're really boring

- You have nothing in common

- They talk a lot and don't listen to you

- They pressure you to do things

- They won't meet your parents or family

- Your values aren't similar

- Your goals are very different

- They won't stop talking about themselves

- They show little or no interest in you

- They try to convert you to their religion

- They don't share your religion

- They talk about their former girl- or boyfriend too much

- They make sexual comments about other people

- They're mean

- They're depressed

- They're hyper

- They're super judgmental

- You just don't like them

Deal breakers are something adults don't even bother to clearly consider when it comes to dating! It seems like such an obvious thing – to know what you will and will not tolerate in a relationship – but most people don't take the time to do this. Because you are doing this at the start of your dating career, you will be on track to have more great dates than bad ones.

Pressure, Pressure, Pressure!

You can feel pressured by your friends, your boy- or girl-friend, or yourself to do all kids of things and most are unrelated to sex and dating. If you are feeling any pressure at all to have sex or do something sexual it's best to wait until you can be wholeheartedly committed to your decision to become sexually active. When it comes to having sex, the only kind of pressure you should feel is to protect yourself and your partner from unplanned pregnancy and STI/HIV.

What kind of pressure to become sexually active are you experiencing?

- Pressure from myself to fit in, get it over with, or because "it's time."

- Pressure from my boyfriend or girlfriend.

- Pressure from my friends.

- Pressure from movies, TV, and other media.

- No pressure at all.

Intuition Is Your Friend

You've probably heard of the "fight or flight response"—the animal instinct that tells us to either do battle or run away if we feel threatened in some way. When you experience this, you have a physical reaction: your adrenaline increases, your palms might get sweaty, your heart may beat faster, and you may have a very strong impulse to run away, or, maybe, smack someone. It can be a strong feeling that is hard to control.

There's another feeling tied to the fight or flight response called "intuition." Your intuition provides you with a very similar set of sensations and feelings, but usually on a smaller scale. This is also called your "gut instinct" or "gut feeling."

Your intuition is one of your best friends in the world of dating and romance. If you can take a minute and pay attention to it, it will rarely steer you wrong. Your gut tells you, if you are willing to listen, when someone isn't safe, if something isn't a good idea, or if you should do something different.

Think of someone you know who kind of gives you the creeps. This could be an adult you know pretty well, like your uncle or best friend's dad, or someone you just see now and again, like the checker at the grocery store.

That creepy, "uh-oh" or uncomfortable feeling you get is your intuition telling you there is something off about that person. It's not a perfect system, but it is accurate nearly all of the time. Sometimes it's because the person is mentally unstable, on drugs or drunk, or because they are "off" in some other way.

If you are out on a date with someone you don't know well and you start to get this feeling, pay attention. It's very tempting to dismiss these feelings because your date may be really cute and charming. If you get that uncomfortable feeling do not dismiss it. Make note, proceed with caution, and think twice about spending any more time than necessary with this person.

Dating Your Friends—Smart Move or Not?

At some point you may find yourself considering dating someone who is already a friend. This can be a smart move because you already know and like them and your friendship can easily blossom into something more. However, if you decide to ask a friend out on a date, make sure it's clear that it's a date. If you only suggest hanging out together, but aren't clear about your intentions (whether this hanging out is a date or not) things can get sticky.

Mateo asked his friend Eve to go to the movies with him and when he went to pick her up he brought her a rose. Smells like a date, right? Roses mean romance in just about every part of the world. It turns out he wasn't sure if he wanted to be romantically involved with her, and at the end of their "not-a-date-date" he decided he wasn't interested in her that way.

She, however, thought they were on a date-date and ended up confused and with hurt feelings and their friendship suffered. Because Mateo wasn't clear in the first place, he ended up ruining a good friendship.

73

If you aren't sure how you feel about someone, please don't do anything that seems romantic if you don't really mean it. Dating a friend can be really smart – just be clear about your intentions.

Sex and Dating: The Two Most Important Things to Know

What should you do if you are already sexually active or are plan to become sexually active? You already know the consequences of having unprotected sex and there are two chapters devoted to sex later in the book. At this point, suffice it to say that the better you know the person, the better the sex.

If sex is in your dating plan, really get to know your partner. Make sure you're comfortable talking about anything and everything before you have sex. If you are too embarrassed to talk about birth control, condoms, or past partners, this is a sure sign that you should probably wait.

There are two big things that should be in place if you decide to have sex or fool around with someone (you kids still say that, right?). If these two simple things are discussed, chances are significantly higher you will have a positive experience:

- **You have an emotional connection.** This means you really like or love your potential partner and tell them. You can say "I really, really like you a lot" if you are not in love with the person (and this is true)!

- **You talk about your relationship status.** This means you talk about whether this means you are now exclusively dating, this was a one-time thing or you are "friends with benefits."

And please make sure you know how to use a condom, where to get them, and carry them with you —both guys and girls. Practice using it with a banana or on yourself so there isn't any trouble in the heat of the moment. Practice makes perfect.

And though your parents are probably freaking out if they are reading this, the bottom line is nearly everyone eventually has sex. It is foolish to think, "it won't happen to me" or for parents to think "my teen won't do it." It's better for everyone if you're prepared to protect yourself when you decide to have sex.

Stuff to Think About!

Have you experienced any of these deal breakers on dates or in your relationships? What would you do differently this time?

What is your plan for handling sexual pressure? Who can you talk to about it?

If you are on a date with someone who is giving you a creepy or uncomfortable feeling, what is your plan for keeping yourself safe?

Have you dated a friend or thought about dating a friend? How did it go? What's your plan for asking your friend out?

CHAPTER EIGHT

Am I Really in Love? It's a Crush! It's Lust! It's Love!

Now that you understand the difference between family, friend, and romantic love, it's easier to understand your feelings when you are dating. We're going to spend time looking at crushes, lust, and falling in love—real "in love" love—in this chapter. These things are tied together, which you know, and one often leads to the next.

Crushes or infatuations are practice for real relationships. They fire us up, spur us on, and get us out the dating door. Crushes can feel really good and fun but can also be confusing and hard, especially when your crush isn't crushing back. Do you remember your first major crush? How does it feel to have a crush on someone - pretty good and a little crazy making, right?

When you have a crush on someone, sometimes there is nothing you can do about it—like when it's a celebrity. Usually though, the person you have a crush on is a real, live person you see regularly.

What should you do about having a crush? Should you ask that person out? Never talk to them and keep them in a safe fantasy bubble? Tell your best friends and then get all weird when your crush is around? Keep it to yourself?

It's pretty much up to you what happens when you have a crush. It can be obvious you have a crush and sometimes it's not so obvious, so proceed with caution. You don't want to look like a fool around this person, so be careful what you say and do and who you tell. Sometimes your friends will "out" your crush, before you are ready. Frankly, this sucks, as I'm sure you probably know or guessed.

Take a minute and think about all those good feelings you have for your crush. Interestingly, a whole bunch of these feelings, including that feeling of desire or lust, are very much what it feels like when you are in love. However, these crush feelings are not true "in love" feelings, partly because they are one-sided and partly because the relationship is mostly in your head.

Here is a list of some crush feelings:

- Excited
- Exhilarated
- Joyful
- Nervous
- Happy
- Delighted
- Blissful
- Energized
- Wonderful
- Strong physical attraction to desire/lust

- Spellbound
- Dreamy
- Out of control
- High
- Flirty
- Panic
- Jealous
- Longing
- Uncertainty
- Uncomfortable

It is really easy to confuse the good crush feelings for falling-in-love feelings because they are mostly the same feelings. The negative feelings (panic, jealous, etc.) usually are not part of falling-in-love and shouldn't be! And, the missing piece with a crush is the other person feeling the same way. It takes two to be really, truly in love.

Is It Lust?

One of the ingredients in the crush/in-love world is lust or sexual desire. Some sexual desire shows up as actual physical feelings you get in your body. It can feel like a surge or a pull or heat and it feels darned good.

You know what I'm talking about if you are a guy, because that old erection thing is a pretty good indicator that you are having some feelings of lust or desire. Girls and women experience similar physical feelings in their clitoris and vagina. It's just not as obvious.

The other part of sexual desire happens in your head. You think and learn about your (potential) beloved and this adds to your feelings of desire for the person. When you see someone you find attractive, you have a physical reaction, an intellectual reaction, and an emotional reaction.

Your reaction depends upon a bunch of stuff, including what's considered to be attractive in your culture, how they look, and your thoughts and feelings about them. Sexual attraction or desire is a very personal thing. The people you find attractive may not be attractive to your friends. This is just fine. If we were all attracted to the same people, there would be very few humans.

You can experience lust without having any kind of relationship with someone. We are wired to reproduce and sexual desire is part of that wiring. This means you can experience feelings of lust for someone for no good reason other than the fact that they are there and attractive to you in some way.

So what's a person to do with all these lusty feelings? You

could act on them, of course, but this is not always the best idea. Here's a list of things you do by yourself to channel that lusty energy into something else.

- Masturbate

- Fantasize

- Exercise

- Meditate or pray

- Draw, paint, or be creative in some way

- Cook or bake

- Read sexy or romantic novels

- Journal or write erotic stories

There is nothing wrong with feeling sexual desire, it's totally normal and natural. It can be distracting and sometimes an-noying so finding some things to do to help manage your feelings until they go away can be helpful. And if you have a willing partner, lucky you, just be clear about your limits and remember, everyone needs to say a clear "yes" to sexual activity.

Is It Love?

You will know when you are falling in love because you will experience all those fabulous crush feelings for your boy-friend or girlfriend and they will be experiencing them as well. The not-so-fabulous crush feelings should not be pre-sent at all, or at just a teeny, tiny level because there will probably be a little bit of uncertainty about the person until you get to know them really well. Here are some additional things you may experience and feel when you are in love:

- Deep emotional connection

- The belief your partner can do no wrong

- Daydreaming about them (but not thinking obsessively about them)

- Enjoying every minute together

- You feel very attractive

- You find your partner to be very attractive

- Smart

- Confident

- Capable

- Super great and kind of "high"

- Valued and important for just being you

No matter what your parents or other adults say, when you are in love, you are in love. Adults have a tendency to forget about their young love. Remind them that they probably felt the same way about someone when they were a teen. You might even ask them if they thought at the time their feelings were real. They will say yes (trust me, I've asked 100's of them). This can be really fun to do, especially if your parents think your love isn't "real."

Your feelings are valid, no matter what your parents or the other adults in your life think. What can you say to your parents if you are in love and they think it's silly? Be nice, unemotional, and to the point—they'll be more likely to listen to you. Also, it won't hurt to bring your beloved around now and then so your parents can get to know them and see what you see in your partner.

As your relationship deepens, those amazing "in love" feelings can fade and become less intense, but also deeper, more enduring, and start feeling more like family love than romantic love. If your relationship is long lasting, and by long lasting, I mean years, not months, you are able to rely on those early feelings to fuel you along and keep you going and committed to the relationship.

How do you define a long-term relationship?

- One month

- Two months

- Three months

- Six months

- One year

- Three years or more

People sometimes have different ideas of what "long term" means and be sure to add this to your list of "getting to know you" questions. It can be a little unsettling to discover that your partner things two months is a long term relationship when you think long term means over a year.

One more point about being in love - your awesome "in love" feelings can also die and take the relationship with them. Most likely this will happen with the majority of your relationships. You meet, get all crazy about someone, things are going great, and then, bam! one or the other of you is over it. It can be sudden, or gradual, but the experience of your first love being your one and only love is really pretty rare.

Sex, Again!

As your relationship deepens, your sexual behavior will advance. It's easy to go from holding hands to making out to having sex, because the more you get to know someone—especially if you are in love with that person — the more likely you are to do it. It is very important to communicate about your limits, birth control, sexual history, and condom use with your partner. And to make sure you discuss those two most important things: Your emotional connection and what it means for your relationship status.

If you can't talk to your partner about your limits and the other things, it probably means you aren't totally, completely comfortable with them. It may mean you don't fully trust them. If you find yourself in this boat, seriously reconsider having sex. Communication is one of the most important parts of being in a healthy relationship. The "are-we-ready-for-sex" conversation should happen before you are in the heat of the moment. Waaay before.

Here's some sex math for you:

Communication + Clarity + Limits + Openness = Better relationship!

Even though the formula is simple, actually having the conversation can be kind of scary and feel weird or overwhelming for some people. Let's break it down a bit:

Communication: Respectfully sharing your thoughts, opinions and beliefs.

Clarity: You understand your values, position, opinion, wants, needs, and desires and can communicate them to your partner. And they can too.

Limits: You understand how far you will go, physically and

are very clear about it. And you respect and understand your partner's limits.

Openness: You can freely and easily talk about your opinions, values, beliefs, limits, etc. And your partner can too.

Better relationship: Hello! Makes sense that your relationship would better if you've got all this covered because there is less chance for misunderstandings, right?

Here's a little example that might help spur you into talking with your partner. Think about a time you had a misunderstanding with your best friend, boy- or girl friend, or one of your parents. Choose one of those times, when, after you started talking about the situation and why you had the misunderstanding, you had one of those "Ooooooh!" moments when the light bulb went on and you suddenly understood why the miscommunication happened.

Remember how good it felt to gain that understanding and have an open and clear conversation? Remember how much closer you felt? Keep in mind the feelings of closeness and connection that happen in moments like this when you are getting ready to talk to your partner about sex. The closeness happens because of clear communication.

Sample Script to Get the "Sexual Communication" Conversation Rolling

Here's a little more help to pave the way for your "sexual communication" conversation. I know, it seems silly to have a script, but I swear, it makes it so much easier to have a tough conversation if you've practiced your side of it a little.

"I want to check in with you about something. I am having a great time hanging out with you and before we go any further physically, I just wanted to talk about it.

I want to tell you that my rule about this is that before we go any further than . . .

- Hand holding

- Cuddling and some kissing

- Making out

- Touching privates (over/under clothes)

- Oral sex

- Anal sex

- We already have . . .

I want to wait until . . .

- We've been dating a month.

- We've been dating three months.

- We've been dating six months.

- We've been dating a year.

- We've been dating . . .

- I'm married.

- I'm in college.

- We're in a deep committed relationship.

- I'm ready and I'll let you know when that is.

What do you think about this? How long do you want to wait?"

You can also ask your partner, "Are you going to be okay with this?" Most likely, they will say "yes." They want to please you and support you, of course. The reality is it's still up to you to stick to your limits and be careful and aware of how far things are going. It's a slippery slope once you get the old hormones rolling with a fun and exciting make out session.

Once you get this conversation started, it will be easier to have it again or to start conversations about other topics. It can also be used as a test to see just how committed your partner is to you. If they don't want to have this conversation, make fun of you, are otherwise disrespectful, or pressure you this should be very concerning to you. If this happens, most likely it means they aren't all that into you. Your intuition will help you with this, so pay attention to it, too.

The truth is having a crush, falling in love, being in love, or merely being "in lust" can all be really confusing. Fun, sure, but confusing, too. This is one of those parts of life that confuses everyone, pretty much always. And this is one of the chapters in this book that can help you be a much more sane and savvy person when you begin your dating life.

Stuff to Think About!

Who do you have a crush on right now? Do they know? What could you do to figure out if they are crushing back?

If you are dating someone how will you know if you are falling in love with them or they with you?

What do you think about having a script for talking to your partner about when you'll be ready for sex and your limits? Do you think you could really have this kind of conversation with someone?

How comfortable would you be using the communicating about sex script? What would it take to make you comfortable enough to have this conversation?

CHAPTER NINE

What's a Healthy Relationship? What You Should Expect

As you may know, half of all marriages end in divorce. You may very well be dealing with the after effects of your own parent's divorce. It may come as no surprise to you that most adults don't know what a healthy relationship looks like. Frankly, most of them wouldn't know one if it bit them in the butt. Count yourself lucky to be getting a little inside info on what makes a healthy relationship so you can make great choices in life and romance.

If you can take this information to heart now, while you are young and not stuck in bad relationship habits and patterns, you will be much more likely to have successful relationships as you get older.

One Tip That May Just Be the Most Important Thing for You to Know!

If you can't be fully yourself with someone, then the relationship will probably never be deep and long lasting. Your boy- or girl friend should feel like your best friend as well as someone you find physically attractive. You should have the level of comfort to say or do anything (like fart) and to be fully who you are at any moment without feeling self-conscious or any fear of judgment.

In her article, "Signs of a Healthy Relationship," dating expert Deborrah Cooper talks about several important elements of a healthy relationship.[8] She does a great job of making this big topic easy to understand, so I've included them here.

Honest Communication

Honest communication is the biggest key to healthy relation-ships and this means you talk about stuff even if you are un-comfortable about it. When you can talk about uncomfortable things, it deepens your relationship. I know I keep harping about this, but it really is one of the most basic and important parts of great relationships.

It takes time to get to a deep level of communication, so don't expect it to happen immediately. Part of honest communica-tion involves trust, which takes time to develop. When you are willing to listen to your partner and tell them your truth in a loving way, your relationship can become more intimate, deeper, and more meaningful.

If you can talk about challenging parts of life, and really, any-thing, with your partner, you are on your way to a healthy re-lationship. If you can't because you aren't comfortable, you think they'll shut you down or ignore you, or you think it's not okay to talk about difficult topics, then your relationship may never become truly intimate or deep.

Which of these topics would you like to talk to your boyfriend or girlfriend about, but feel uncomfortable to you?

- Politics

- Religion

- Vegetarianism or veganism

- Grades

- Clothes

- Your financial situation

- Body odor

- Bad breathe

- Eating disorders

- Masturbation

- Oral and/or anal sex

- Same sex relationships
- Values
- Abortion
- Different tastes in music, books, movies, etc.
- Bisexuality
- Fantasies
- College
- Post high-school plans
- Divorce

- Death
- Your family life
- Sexual abuse
- Rape
- Physical abuse
- Emotional abuse
- Verbal abuse
- Your past
- Your dreams
- Sexually Transmitted Infections (STIs)

Respect and Thoughtfulness

The word "respect" comes up over and over again when people talk about relationships. Respect means a couple of things. The first is a sense of the worth or excellence of a person. The second has to do with the idea that everyone has certain rights or privileges and these should be accepted. This means we should listen fully, consider the other person's position and opinion, be supportive, and treat them the same way we'd like to be treated. We should also respect their boundaries.

Here are some things you can do that are respectful of your partner:

- Listen carefully and without judgment.

- Consider your partner's likes and dislikes.

- Be helpful.

- Compliment them.

- Say "please" and "thank you."

- Be affectionate, playful, and caring.

- Notice their moods.

- Remember to consider their needs and desires. If they are different than yours, learn how to compromise.

Acceptance

Everyone wants to be accepted and loved for who they are—good and bad; strange and wonderful; whole and damaged. If you cannot accept who your partner is, then they're probably not the person for you.

If you are constantly try to change them or convince them they are wrong for their belief system, liking something or someone you don't, or for taking part in an activity they like, you most likely don't accept your partner for who they are. This kind of behavior can be considered emotionally abusive, which can be just as painful as physical abuse.

Imagine what it's like when someone you love wants you to change something about yourself that you like and are fine with. Not such a great feeling, huh? Acceptance is part of a healthy relationship. You may not like everything your boy- or girlfriend does (this is normal), but if you absolutely can't stand something they do, like, or believe, then it might be time to rethink the relationship.

Trust

This is something that takes time to build. It doesn't happen instantly because you need to have some experiences with a person before you know if you can trust them. Some ways you may know that your boyfriend or girlfriend is trustworthy are:

- You are able to be vulnerable with them and tell your secrets and they keep them to themselves.

- If you say "stop" they stop.

- You can rely on them to do what they say they will do.

- You are relaxed around them and can be fully yourself.

- They have shown you they respect you.

- You have a fight and they stick it out with you until you have a resolution.

- They don't mind spending time with your family and friends.

Boundaries

Part of trust in a relationship has to do with respecting each other's boundaries. Boundaries can be sexual, social, and emotional. Sexual boundaries are obvious—just how far are you willing to go physically?

Social boundaries have to do with the kind of activities you do together: where you go, who you are with, public displays of affection, frequency of texting and phone calling, drinking and drug use, etc. An example of inappropriate social boundaries is when your new boy- or girlfriend texts you 500 times a day, at all hours of the day and night. He or she wants to know where you are and what you are doing and who you are with ALL THE TIME. Is it truly necessary to text this much? Not so much.

Emotional boundaries are things like getting to know each other's likes and dislikes, learning about each other's childhood, talking about challenges in your lives, discussing family dynamics, religious beliefs, politics, and, most importantly, feelings. Getting to know someone takes time, so baring your soul on your first date—telling all the sad and sorry details of your last relationship, why your former love is a giant poop, and all about your traumatic childhood—isn't a good way to go. Too much personal information too soon makes most people feel uncomfortable.

You need to be clear about *your* boundaries first so you can set limits for yourself and communicate them with your partner. This is one of the things this book is for— to help you discover your boundaries. If your boundaries are more flexible than your partner's, things can get challenging because you may be tempted to pressure your partner to do something they aren't ready to do. As we've discussed, pressure isn't okay. The more you show that you respect them, the sooner you can get to know, love, and trust each other even more.

Relationship Feelings

It is important to notice how you feel when you are with your boyfriend, girlfriend, or even someone you are crushing on. Following are lists of good relationship feelings and not-so-good relationship feelings.

Take a moment and think about your current love interest or, if you don't have one now, someone from your past or even your future. Without thinking about it too much, go through the list below and pay attention to the first and strongest feelings that come to mind when you think about being with this person.

Good Relationship Feelings

- Excited
- Relaxed
- Happy
- Confident
- Accepted for who I am
- Blissful
- Wonderful
- Energized
- Strong physical attraction (lust)
- Smart
- Kind
- Beautiful/Handsome
- Sexy
- Caring
- Open
- Comfortable
- Important
- Funny (ha-ha, not odd)
- Needed
- Trusting
- Honest
- Communicative

Not-so-good relationship feelings

- Anxious
- Nervous
- Weird
- Scared
- Ugly
- Bored
- Stupid
- Fat
- Mean
- Uneasy

- Sad
- Jealous
- Uncomfortable
- Unimportant

- Weak
- Trapped
- Confused
- No physical attraction

Now, compare your lists of feelings. If your positive feelings outweigh the negative, bravo! If the negatives outweigh the positives, it's seriously time to reconsider the relationship. Are the feelings basically equal? Keep a close eye on your feelings and consider getting help or leaving the relationship if the negative feelings become stronger.

Healthy relationships feel good nearly all the time. Of course you will have disagreements and bad feelings sometimes, but these should only happen occasionally and certainly not as the main part of the relationship. If you don't feel good in your relationship consider leaving. Find someone to talk to who can help you sort out how you are feeling and whether it is a good idea to stay. Your friends will be helpful, as will your trusted adults.

Relationship Styles[9]

Here is a very simple way of looking at three basic kinds of relationships. Each letter (yes, the actual letter) gives a little picture of these relationship styles. What is your relationship letter? What kind of relationship appeals to you the most?

A Notice how each side will fall without the other's support? They are connected but have lots of dependence on each other, with good reason: one side will collapse without the other.

I I Notice how each side is totally separate and has nothing to do with the other. There is no connection between the sides.

H In this kind of relationship, each side is connected, but can stand on it's own. Each partner can move on from the relationship if needed, without collapse.

If your partner tells you they will "die" without you, they are over dependent and you are probably in an "**A**" relationship. If your partner doesn't want to know about you, support you or you feel like they really don't care all that much about you, this is an example of an "**I I**" relationship.

Strive for an "**H**" relationship because this is the best style of relationship. This relationship is well balanced and there is dependence and independence in equal measure. This means you can do things together or apart. You both have your own friends and friends you share. You support your partner's life and interests and they support yours. Your lives are well connected, but not to the point where you can't function without the other.

List of Behaviors to Worry About

Sometimes your relationship will start out feeling great and then slowly fall apart. Relationships can get ugly. People say and do mean-spirited things, make bad choices (like cheating), and generally do dumb things.

Following is a list of behaviors that should make you worry. Some of these behaviors might also make your "deal breaker" list. If you are in a relationship and are experiencing any of the things on this list, it may be time to reconsider whether to stay in the relationship. Talk to someone about what's going on and don't be afraid to get some help if you need it.

- Controlling—they tell you what to wear, where to go,

who you can hang out with, what to eat, when to eat, what music to listen to, etc.

- He or she is more than three years older than you. An older person can pressure a younger person into doing something they normally wouldn't do with someone their age. The bigger the age difference, the more likely you will be to have sex.

- Pressure you to have sex or go physically further than you are comfortable.

- Their values clearly don't mesh with yours.

- Talk only about themselves and never ask you anything about yourself.

- Violence of any kind. (There's more information on this in the next chapter.)

- Threatening violence—they threaten to hurt you, themselves, or someone else.

- They are consistently late, don't show up or change plans.

- Call, text, or e-mail other people and/or you obsessively.

- Forwards naked or sexual pictures of you to other people (this is illegal).

- Requests you send them naked pictures of yourself (this is illegal, too).

- Send naked or sexual pictures of themselves to you (once again, illegal).

- Are verbally abusive (say you are stupid, ugly, worthless, etc.).

- Your friends and or parents hate him/her—seriously, pay attention to this!

- Lie to you or ask you to lie for them.

- Do drugs or drink in a way that feels uncomfortable to you.

- Drink or do other drugs and drive.

- Ditch you to be with their friends.

- Do anything that you don't like or are uncomfortable with (trust your gut!).

- Insist you do things you don't feel comfortable doing (sex, drugs, drinking, lying for them, etc.).

Here's a real life example: Danny had just started dating Julie and after their first date she started saying bad and mean things about his friends. She told him they were stupid and said he wasn't allowed to hang out with them any more. She also hit him in the face because he told her to stop being mean and telling him what to do. Danny immediately broke up with her. She then started posting lies and other things about him on Facebook. He unfriended her.

Can you spot the red flags? I figured you could. Even though he knew her behavior was wrong, he was still unsure about how he handled it and checked in with me to make sure he was on the right track in dealing with her craziness. I assured him he was and suggested he have his friends keep an eye on her Facebook posts to make sure she was being appropriate. We then agreed that if she had not stopped, he would talk to his parents.

When you understand what makes a healthy relationship, it can make it easier for you to notice when you are in a situation that isn't good for you. It also gives you something to measure your relationships against, rather than trying to figure it out on your own.

Stuff to Think About!

What would it take for you to be fully your "real" self with your partner, friends or family?

Are you in an **A**, **H** or **I I** relationships? What about your friends? **A**, **H** or **I I**? What do you think about these relationship styles?

What has changed about your understanding of healthy relationships as a result of reading this chapter?

Do you know someone who is in an unhealthy relationship? What could you do to help them? What would you want them to do for you if you were in an unhealthy relationship?

CHAPTER TEN

When Should I End It? Signs to Know It's Time to Go

You probably don't want to think or talk about dating violence or sexual abuse. However, if you're going to be a savvy, healthy dater, you need to buck up and consider some of these things. The more you know, the better you will feel about your choices, your partner, and your dating life in general. You'll also be able to help your friends if they are experiencing any kind of abuse in their relationships.

Dating Violence

Dating violence is a big problem among teens, so it's important for you to know the warning signs. Some statistics say that one in three teens will experience violence in their dating relationships.[10] Dating violence knows no boundaries: it can happen to anyone, no matter your racial, religious, or ethnic background; rich, poor, and in between; it can happen to you whether you are in a heterosexual or same sex relationship.

"Dating violence" means one or both persons in a dating, non-married relationship threatens violence or actually performs an act of violence towards the other. Violence does not just include physical acts such as hitting, slapping, shoving, or forced sex. It can also be emotional or verbal abuse, too.

Dating violence can be sneaky. You can be in a relationship and think that things are moving along well. Over the course of time, however, you may find yourself feeling bad about yourself, unhappy, unsure, or afraid of your partner.

There are a number of reasons you may not notice (or want to believe) that your relationship is unhealthy. Some of it has to do with your family life or your youth and inexperience. You just haven't been on the planet long enough to fully understand how human relationships work. Some of it has to do with the massive amount of media you've eaten up over the years.

Movies and TV shows make romance and dating look like this sexy and fun thing, and even if there's trouble of some sort there is nearly always some kind of happy ending. Maybe the trouble is minimal, like a fight or a misunderstanding, or maybe it's something big, like abuse or a pregnancy. Regardless, the characters either kiss and make up, someone comes to the rescue, or the misunderstanding is cleared up and all is well in the end.

Even if the relationship might not make it, everything works out just fine. Right? Lots of teens think that their dating life should be just like the movies— super romantic, sexy, and fun.

I hate to break it to you, but your life is not a movie.

So, what the heck does this have to do with dating violence? Here's the deal, dating violence is very confusing, especially if it happens in your first relationships. Your excitement about having a boy- or girlfriend may make it so you put up with a bunch of stuff that isn't good for you.

All those media message about what a "normal" relationship should be like can also influence you. You may be so charmed by your partner you excuse the behavior, ignore it, or decide their behavior is your fault. It's not! Chances are good they will not change their behavior, no matter how hard you try to change yours to please them.

Here are some early warning signs that your date (or you)

may eventually become abusive:[10, 11]

- Extreme jealousy

- Controlling behavior

- Quick involvement—after two days they are madly in love with you

- Unpredictable mood swings

- Alcohol and/or drug use; excessive gaming

- Explosive anger

- Keeps you away from friends and family

- Doesn't like your friends and family and vice versa

- Uses force during an argument

- Shows hypersensitivity—you tease them and they freak out

- Believes in rigid gender roles—for example, only guys should ask girls out and not the other way around

- Blames others for his or her problems or feelings

- Cruel to animals or children

- Verbally abusive

- Name-calling

- Threatens violence

- Not tolerant of your culture or religion

- You don't feel good, safe or respected when you're with them

If you aren't sure about your situation or any of these things seem familiar, please talk to a trusted adult or friend about your concerns or call one of the hotlines in the resources section at the back of this book to get support and information.

The Cycle of Violence[12]

Dating violence often shows up as a cycle in a relationship. Here's what usually happens in a relationship caught up in the cycle of violence:

Honeymoon phase: Everything is wonderful; you're having fun, falling in love, and feel great!

The relationship deepens: You share more about yourself with your partner, good feelings still abound.

Some kind of violence happens: A slap, mean comment, controlling behavior, jealousy, sexual behavior you're not ready for, etc. This can happen very early in the relationship or later.

Big apology: Promises to change behavior, respect your boundaries, to never be violent again, etc.

Honeymoon phase again: By this time you may feel nervous, unsure, and start feeling bad about yourself.

Smooth-ish sailing: You might feel a little uncertain about your partner or your relationship.

Some kind of violence happens again: A slap, mean comment, controlling behavior, etc.

Bigger apology: Promises to change behavior, respect your boundaries, to never be violent again, etc.

Honeymoon phase again: Honeymoons are shorter and more and more uncomfortable.

The cycle repeats itself: There are shorter amounts of time between incidents and honeymoons.

Eventually there may be violence all the time: You may feel constantly "on guard" and afraid of your partner.

What's important here is that it doesn't feel good to be in a relationship with this person. The cycle may happen quickly, slowly, or off and on. You may recognize this in your own relationship, your parents', or even a friend's. If you do see this cycle in anyone's relationship, it can be helpful to talk to someone so you can have some support and make a plan to get or give help.

You are probably wondering at what point you should leave the relationship if this happens to you. The minute you entertain the idea of leaving the relationship, you should. Chances are very slim it will get better. When you leave you send a strong message you won't put up being treated this way which is important because it may inspire your former partner get support and help.

Maybe you are wondering why anyone would stay in a relationship like this at all. Abusive relationships are complicated, and there really isn't a good answer. Fear plays a big role in not leaving the relationship because the victim often has become very afraid of their partner and very unsure of themselves.

Talking to your friends or a trusted adult can be a good reality check and help you understand whether the relationship is healthy. If someone you trust tells you they are worried about your relationship, don't get defensive. They will also probably be someone who can help you leave if you need to.

How to Talk to Your Partner if They Do Something You Don't Like

Be very clear about what it is you don't like and tell them as soon as it happens. If you don't like it when they text while you're talking to them, tell them. If you don't like it when they pinch you on the butt "for fun" tell them. If you don't like it when they order you around, tell them. Get it?

Ask them to stop the behavior and let them know it bothers you/hurts your feelings/makes you feel afraid or whatever is true for you. You can say, "Sweetie, when you order me around like a drill sergeant, I feel annoyed because I think it's disrespectful. I am not your servant, I'm your sugar-pie!"

Decide what you will do if the behavior doesn't stop or change. You can decide to leave if they do it again. You can take a break from the relationship. Confide in a trustworthy friend or adult and ask them to look out for you and help you stick to your decision, if need be. Ask them to help you make a game plan.

If you ask them to stop, and the behavior continues, you may have some trouble on your hands. Check in with someone you trust so you can have a different perspective. If your gut or intuition tells you this isn't okay, trust yourself. Find some help and support.

Although you may think you will be with whomever you are dating forever, teenage relationships are usually practice for the relationships you will have as an adult, and most likely won't be long-term. Knowing the signs of trouble and how and when to leave a bad relationship NOW are skills and knowledge you will carry with you throughout your lifetime.

Sexual Abuse

Sexual abuse is something that is really hard to talk about, and you will probably feel pretty uncomfortable reading about it. This is normal. If you have been sexually abused by someone, or have sexually abused another person, it can be helpful to talk to someone about what's happened to you. You can call the Rape, Abuse and Incest National Network right now and talk to someone anonymously (see resources section).

Nearly all of the time, teens are abused by someone they know. The abuser is usually someone who should be trustworthy, like a parent, stepparent, cousin, coach, teacher, pastor, priest, stepsibling, sibling, family friend, neighbor, uncle, aunt, or babysitter. Someone from school, a friend of a friend, or a boyfriend or girlfriend can also be sexually abusive. Most often it is a man, although women can sexually abuse as well. When sexual abuse happens between immediate family members it's called incest.

Often, teens don't know that they are being abused because the abuser is so tricky and sneaky. They spend time getting to know you and your family, developing your parents' and your trust. Then they can slowly start to "groom" you into being their victim. The victim feels flattered and special because of the attention and the special relationship they have with the abuser. These good feelings are hard to separate from the bad stuff that is going on. Or, sometimes the abuse happens once, very quickly and never happens again.

The offender can use drugs and alcohol as a tool to sexually assault their victim. For example, they give someone a strong drink or go to a party and monitor who is highly intoxicated and then pick that person to abuse.

Here's a definition of sexual abuse: pressuring or tricking another person into sexual activity for one's own pleasure. Besides sexual touching, it includes non-touching things such as:

- Someone exposing their penis or other private body parts (exhibitionism)

- Showing someone pornography

- Being spied on (voyeurism)

- Communicating in a sexual way by phone, text or online

If any of this has happened to you or is happening to you, it is important to know three things:

1. It's absolutely not your fault.

2. Teens can and do recover.

3. Your abuser needs help and knows what they are doing is wrong.

Sexual abuse can be an agonizing and traumatic experience for its victims. It can also feel good, even though you know there is something wrong about the relationship. There are many places to get help. You just need to ask. If you tell someone and they don't believe you, tell someone else. It is probably easiest to tell a good friend first and then ask them to support you when you tell an adult.

It will be helpful to have someone you trust with you as you go through this process. You will need to be very brave to tell about the abuse and it may be one of the scariest things you've ever done, but you can do it. And if you can't do it for yourself, do it for the next kid this person will target.

Sometimes, kids will fool around with other kids, "playing doctor" or other games that involve some sexual touch, like Spin-the-Bottle or Truth or Dare.[13] Usually, this is considered normal behavior for children. Kids learn about their sexual selves through play and curiosity. If you have bad feelings about this from your own experience or if someone forced or manipulated you into playing this way, you may have been sexually abused.

Sometimes parents find kids playing this way and completely freak out when there is nothing to be freaked out about. If this happened to you, and you are traumatized because of your parents' behavior, not your own, you probably have nothing to worry about.

No matter what, if you feel bad in some way about something that happened to you as a child, it's a good idea to talk to someone about it. You don't need to suffer alone – an outrageous number of people were sexually abused or had other traumatic experiences as children and it's 100% possible to recover and lead a happy and healthy life.

If you have sexually abused someone (or think you may have), there is help for you, too. The sooner you ask for it, the better the likelihood you will recover. *Stop It Now!* is an organization that works with offenders and you can call them and talk to someone anonymously. You can find their info in the Resources section.

Talking about Sex in Your Relationship

In healthy relationships, partners are able talk to each other about their sexual limits, respect each other's boundaries, and get consent every time they have sex or engage in a sexual activity. Consent means permission. There should be a clear understanding that the activity is okay with both partners. Everyone needs to say "yes" to the activity and if one person has been drinking or using drugs, they can't consent.

Knowing what a healthy relationship looks like (and doesn't) is a life skill. Because you've read this chapter, you are well on your way to making good decisions about your relationships and getting help if you need it.

Stuff to Think About!

What are some warning signs you will look out for in your relationships?

Is there something your partner does that you don't like? What can you say to them?

Do you know anyone that is experiencing dating violence? What can you do to help them?

Sexual abuse can be really hard to talk and think about. If you have been sexually abused, or know someone who has been, what is one thing you can do to take steps towards getting help?

CHAPTER ELEVEN

Are You Ready for Sex?
Part 1: The Emotional Stuff (Mostly)

This is the big question, isn't it? Are you ready for sex? Really, only you know the answer. Most parents say that teens aren't ready for sex until they're out of high school or in college. The reality is that most teens have sex for the first time at about seventeen—which isn't to say that all of you are having sex at this age, some are doing it earlier and some later[14].

The Longer You Wait, the Better the Sex!

The smartest, safest thing to do—for both your emotional health and your physical health—is to wait as long as possible before you have sex for the first time. The more mature you are, the better the sex. You can ask any adult who was sexually active as a teen and they will tell you that sex later in life is better. This is because you will be more ready to handle the consequences, more likely to protect yourself, and you will be more confident about your body and your bedroom skills. Seriously, waiting is smarter.

You probably know people who have had sex, some who haven't, and some who lie about it. You probably know someone who has an "everything but" policy or will engage in oral or anal sex, but not vaginal intercourse. You probably know someone who has never even held hands with someone, let alone kissed them. And you probably know someone who's made out with people and that's about it. And one of those "someones" may be you.

Every type of sexual activity is going on out there and your job is to know what feels right to you, what your sexual values are, and where your boundaries lie. Having read this far, you should be feeling pretty clear about your values and boundaries. By the way, this is a lifelong process, so don't think you should have it all completely figured out right now. Most adults are still trying to figure this out!

What the Heck Is "Sex" Anyway?

Sex can mean vaginal intercourse (penis in vagina), but there are other things that are considered sex as well - oral sex (penis/vaginal area in mouth) and anal sex (penis in anus), for example. Sex is part of their names, after all, so this makes it easy to know these things are considered "sex."

Sex is really much more than these three things. Most of the time when people talk about "sex," what they mean is this: Any activity with part of one person's body and another person's "privates" that involves possible exchange of body fluids, like semen or vaginal secretions.

But really, it's a fluid and ever changing definition, for society and for the individual because there are so many things people can do that are sexual. Kissing, hugging, body rubbing, and masturbating together are some of the things. You need to decide for yourself what your limits are and then talk to your partner about this. And they need to respect your limits and vice versa. End of story.

Even if you've already had sex, you can still have a plan that will help you decide if your current or future partner is worthy of being physically intimate with you. Just because you've done it before, doesn't mean you have to do it again.

How I Lost It! Tales about Losing Virginity

Every sexually active person has a story about how they lost their virginity and this is a story that will stick with you throughout your life. As you read through the true stories that follow, pay attention to the parts of the stories that feel right to you and the parts that don't. These stories are universal. If you'd like to read more loss of virginity stories, there's a great blog *The Virginity Project* that has tons of them. The web address is listed in the resources section.

Gabe's Story—The Timing Felt Right

It was the summer of my sophomore year in high school, and I was just about to turn seventeen. I had been dating a girl for the better part of a month, and we both knew we were very close—there was something unique in our connection.

She wasn't a virgin and she had been with a couple of boyfriends before me, which I kind of found intimidating. That, along with the pressure from my friends and my own desires, was compounding the tension of the situation.

Her mom worked during the day, so we would hang out at her place and relax. We fooled around a lot and we could both sense what was going to happen— that we would eventually go all the way.

It was one of the hottest days of the year, about mid-July. I had no idea how to approach the subject, so I decided to just see what would happen if I said, "I don't have a condom, but we could still . . . " and before I could finish my sentence, we were in her room. She was on the pill, so we weren't worried about her getting pregnant.

It was very quick, but very passionate. I felt a sense of relief and also a sense that I was closer to her. However, when I went home that day, I was very confused. Although this had been exactly what I wanted, I still questioned the experience. I wasn't sure if what I had done was right, if somehow I had cheated myself.

Eventually, I realized that it had been a meaningful and special experience for both of us, and that there was no reason to feel guilty. Overall, it was a good experience, but if I do have one piece of advice, it would be to choose a much cooler day to loose your virginity. Regardless of how special it was, 100 plus degree weather makes for messy sex!

Katherine's Story—I Waited Until I Was Twenty-One

I had a serious boyfriend from high school through the first few years of college—he's my husband now. Over the years, we did plenty sexually and had a fantastic intimate life together, although we steered clear from actual sexual intercourse.

I had learned my lesson about pregnancy in middle school, and wasn't about to have it happen to me. I remember when the girl sitting next to me in orchestra showed me her ultrasound picture. She was in seventh grade! I knew at that moment that I didn't need any of that. When I met Ken—my husband—in high school, his Christian upbringing had led him to believe that sex was a sacred thing for committed married people.

So . . . on to college. My junior year (Ken didn't go to the same college so we were geographically separated) I decided I wanted to test the waters and broke up with Ken—and broke his heart in a million pieces. I ended up dating a guy named Wade, for more than a year and eventually, we decided it was time. He still lived at home, and his parents didn't mind when I would spend the night. I remember feeling pretty good about it, in general. I had had enough experience getting up to that "exact moment" and felt I had the skills.

But at the very moment he entered me, I started to cry. He was genuine and thoughtful and asked a few nice questions and I told him it was my first time. I think he was astounded on the one hand and eager on the other. It went fine but I could tell he had much more experience than I did and afterwards I asked him how much exactly.

His answer shocked me and made me feel like I was quite behind schedule for my age, but I just rolled over and obsessed (for what seemed like hours) about the number of people he had had sex with—seven.

We stayed together for a while afterward, but it didn't take me long to realize there wasn't much more to the relationship. Regularly we had sex before he got up to go to work in the morning and then I would lay there, after he was gone, thinking about how bizarre this all was.

Every morning I had "the walk of shame" through his mother's kitchen while his father was sitting in his home office. Weird thing was that I was the one who felt awkward and ashamed; everything seemed pretty normal to them.

I have always been happy that I waited so long. I suppose I'm happy my first time was with Wade, but there's definitely a part of me that wonders whether I should have waited longer.

I can't imagine having done it earlier in my life: I can't even imagine how that would have gone. It was such an emotional thing for me when I was twenty-one, I can't even fathom going through those emotions when I was eighteen, fourteen, or twelve. I can't even imagine it.

Talia's Story—I Got It Over With

I lost my virginity at fourteen because I thought my friend was also doing it in the other room. I was with a boy I didn't care about and who didn't care about me. Even though I didn't want to have sex, I did it anyway because I thought lots of girls at school had already done it.

113

Afterwards, I found out that my friend didn't do it and that the rumors at school, mostly, weren't true. I hated myself for a long time and it took me a long time to forgive myself. Even after that, I had my first real boyfriend at fifteen and had sex with him only because I thought I had to in order to keep him.

I was having sex for two years even though I didn't want to. Looking back, I think that because I didn't have a good relationship with my parents when I became a teenager, I was looking for a connection with boys to compensate for it.

I hated sex for a long time because of my early experiences. I came from a good family— the "perfect family" to other people we knew. My parents never talked to me about sex, or drugs, or how to say "no." I learned everything from kids at school and TV.

Julian's Story—It Was a Gift

I was a junior in high school, and my girlfriend was a senior. We had met during a drama production and had been dating for two or three months. We fell in love with each other and things had been getting progressively more intimate.

The evening of my sixteenth birthday, she told me she had talked to her mother and gotten birth control and that we should do it. She was also a virgin and wanted to give me this for my birthday present. I said: "Okay!"

That night, we went downstairs to her bedroom and had sex for the first time. I'm not sure if her parents were home, but they definitely knew what was up. We continued to have sex at her house nearly every day after school until she went to college.

Jessica's Story—I Was Engaged

I'm one of those pretty rare birds—I think—who didn't actually have much romance in her life in high school or college. I would describe my personality as "pretty shy socially" yet driven to excel in school, sports, etc.

There never seemed to be time for relationships, and aside from a few dates, things never progressed from there. In my junior year of college I did a work trip on a sailboat and happened to meet a great guy who was the captain of the boat. I had left something on the boat—a coffee cup, no less—which he returned to me with a cute little letter.

I wrote back and we spent the latter part of that year writing letters to one another. The following year things had progressed to a few dates and a first kiss. By the time I was ready to graduate from college we had determined that we were madly in love so I proposed to him!

I was a virgin, but had not really thought too much about what my values were. Honestly, I just think the right guy had never come along. It had never been my intention to lose my virginity on my honeymoon. I think we were both assuming that we'd wait until then, but I began thinking to myself that it seemed silly to wait and I wanted to "practice" for our honeymoon.

So, we did our "practicing" which was immensely fun for the months leading up to the wedding. When I think back on it, I feel grateful that things happened on my terms. The idea of "practicing" to have sex made it feel like there was no pressure, since we could just move forward, explore, and see where things led.

Mathew's Story—I Was Drunk

I was seventeen and lived in a small town. I had had girlfriends and dated quite a few girls, but had never had sex with any of them. One night I went out with one of my sister's friends, Anna. She was fourteen, I think. We went to a party where everyone was hanging out and someone had beer, so we were drinking.

I got drunk (and she did, too) and we started to make out in a bedroom. One thing led to another and I ended up having sex with her. I remember thinking when we were making out, "I think she'll have sex with me! May as well get this out of the way." So we did. I kind of pressured her into it. I think we used a condom, so that was good. I really have no idea if she really wanted to have sex, or did it because she was drunk or what. And I never found out because we didn't go out again.

At the time, losing my virginity really wasn't that big of a deal to me. I was relieved to have it "out of the way." But now I think it sort of set me up to look at sex as something casual and not really that important. I feel bad about taking advantage of Anna—and being drunk. It was stupid.

Lillie's Story—I Was at Camp

I was fifteen; he was fourteen. He was gorgeous and he was my best guy friend. We were just hanging out one afternoon and he started touching my breast —completely out of the blue. I asked him what he was doing and he asked me if I wanted to "goof around." I said, "Sure . . ."—and was wowed because this amazing guy liked me!

We kept fooling around for a couple days after that— exploring stuff. Then the weekend arrived, and we were both going to church camp. Somehow, he had a room to himself so we planned on getting together at some point.

I told someone who was a good friend that we had been fooling around, and then she told someone else, who told his older sister, who then told his mother. She was pissed at him, and he was very pissed at me, so I thought nothing would happen over the weekend.

I was totally surprised—and completely flattered—when he approached me and he still wanted to have sex or even fool around with me, even though he was really mad. It made me feel giddy, and I sort of thought that he'd forgiven me for telling and we would still be friends.

I thought this was the absolute perfect situation: he was gorgeous, I trusted him, and we were really, really good friends—after all, he still wanted to fool around with me. I was scared, but I trusted him.

We finally found the right time to sneak into his room together. I had no idea how big an erect penis was—I'd never seen one. When he started to put it in, we weren't lying down, we were standing up, and it wasn't easy. I seized up, and it would only go in a little bit, and I told him to stop. He did and we didn't go any further. After that, he told me he was going to get "blue balls." *

He ignored me the rest of the weekend and flirted with several other girls, which really hurt my feelings. He pretty much never talked to me again. I regret my decision to this day because it led me to distrust men and for the longest time made it really, really hard to have intimate relationships. I thought men only wanted to use me for sex, that they didn't care about my feelings, and that they wanted to humiliate me.

*Guys tell girls that they'll get "blue balls" if they don't have sex and/or ejaculate. The idea is that their balls will explode. This is not true. They might feel that way, and have some pain, but it's not going to happen. They can take care of themselves if they really need to.

Araceli's Story—I Found Out I Was a Lesbian

I lost my virginity a few days before my twentieth birthday. I had gone on a date with an old high-school flame who had been away at college. (I had stayed in my hometown attending the local community college.) During the evening he asked if I still was a virgin. After talking about sex for a while, he confessed he was still a virgin, too.

He asked me if I was interested in having sex so we could both say we had "done it" and get on with the rest of our lives, having put this one behind us. Somehow, this made sense to me. I had been putting guys off long enough. Here was a friend, a safe playmate, who better to do it with?

I remember we had this discussion languishing in his parents' hot tub while they weren't home. We couldn't do it there. It didn't seem right. I had driven over in my ever-dependable station wagon. We thought the car would work.

We climbed out of the hot tub, dried off, and—without socks and underwear —drove up into the hills outside of town. It was dark and I don't remember exactly where we stopped, but we felt safe enough to stop, park, get in the back, put the seats down, and start making out. This foreplay inevitably led to both of our first experience with sexual intercourse.

We played it off like a grand experiment. We went slow. He checked in with me at every stop. I asked him how "that" felt, "what if we . . . how about that?" He had taken a condom from his father's underwear drawer so at least we were safe.

He climaxed. I just experienced it. After all was said and done, I found myself vaguely disappointed. Was this all there was? Huh. So that is the big deal?

The next day, I plopped myself on the kitchen counter while my mom was making dinner. I said "Well, I finally had sex last night and it wasn't such a big deal like everyone makes it out to be." My mother (only slightly shocked) replied, "Maybe it was just the situation. When you have it with the right person it will be different."

118

The next time it was with the right person—or so I thought—but it didn't seem that much different. I tried a few more times, still the same. It just wasn't that great. And I did have very good lovers.

I didn't have a satisfying—both physically and spiritually—experience until two years later, while I was away at college. This time it was with a woman. My Catholic Latina upbringing was shook to its foundation.

For almost seven years I struggled with self-acceptance, my family, my religion, and—most important—my identity. It took many years of annual "water testing" to conclude I was gay and to love myself again. My mother later confessed she knew something was very different about me when I so gleefully shared my "first time" experience with her.

She was right.

Kara's Story—I Did It with My First Love

I met Tim through a mutual friend when I was fifteen. He was sixteen, and lived about a half-hour drive from me, but we somehow managed to see each other once a week. He was just a really cool person—a wacky, totally uninhibited musician whose band played local gigs regularly.

Tim showered me with love and affection, both publicly and privately. He wrote songs for me and pulled me on stage to slow dance while he performed. He'd find the ugliest underwear in my dresser drawer and write notes all over it with a Sharpie about how beautiful and sexy I was. In short, he made me feel special.

He was also much more direct and open about sex than any other boy I'd been with, and certainly more than my family was. Tim was my first love, and I was pretty convinced I'd be with him for the rest of my life. It made perfect sense that he be my first.

I decided that sixteen was the perfect time to lose my virginity. We made plans to meet late at night on my birthday. I spent the night at a friend's house, snuck out around ten o'clock, and met Tim at a baseball park.

We chose a spot near third base and spread out blankets, huddling beneath them to keep warm (it was March in Northern California). We had the condom all ready. There was just one problem: Tim couldn't get an erection. We tried to stuff his penis inside me anyway, but that didn't work.

Finally, we gave up and decided we'd try it another time when we could find a warmer, more comfortable location. Later we joked that we might have had more success had we set up our love nest on home plate.

A better opportunity came a week later, when my parents were out for the day. We used my bed, and Tim had no problems getting an erection this time. What I remember mainly is how much it hurt—the stinging, the jabbing at my insides, and a little bit of blood.

Even though it was not Tim's first time, he was ecstatic to have helped me lose my virginity. Afterwards, we swam in my pool and giggled whenever I winced at the pain between my legs.

I felt proud of the pain; it represented a huge transition in my life. I was no longer a virgin. I was a sexually active young woman. My new status would prove to be both a privilege and a huge responsibility.

Things to Think About Before You Have Sex

If you think you might be ready to have sex, here is a list of some things you might want to ask yourself before you take the plunge. One important thing to remember: once you be-come sexually active, it's really hard to say "no" to continued sexual activity.

"Am I Ready" Checklist

Some of these questions call for a yes-or-no answer and some require more thought. Only you can decide if the time is right and this list should help you become clearer about your deci-sion. You have to decide—consciously decide—what is best for you and then do your darnedest to stick to your decision.

- Do I love or like my partner and does he/she love or like me just as much? Have we discussed this?

- Have we discussed with this means for our relation-ship afterwards?

- Does my partner agree this is the next step in our rela-tionship and is this a truly mutual decision?

- Am I feeling any pressure at all from myself, my friends, or my partner to become sexually active?

- Am I looking forward to this experience?

- Have I consciously thought through my choice and am I making a planned decision?

- Do I have open communication with my partner and can we talk about anything, including birth control, condom use, and future plans?

- Is this clearly my choice?

- Do I have condoms and know how to use them? Have I discussed using condoms with my partner?

- Am I comfortable carrying or buying condoms?

- Have I discussed birth control with my partner?

- Do I, or my partner, have birth control and know how to use it?

- Am I in a safe and healthy relationship?

- Can I talk about my feelings with my partner?

- Am I doing this to keep my partner?

- Do I understand how to give my partner pleasure?

- Will I feel guilty or have any regrets afterwards?

- Have we discussed our sexual histories, including whether we've ever had an STI? And, if necessary, have we been tested for STIs and/or HIV?

- What role will alcohol and drugs play in this decision? By the way, although alcohol and drugs can lower your self-consciousness, they can also make you forget to use, or not care about using, a condom!

- If I get an STI or HIV am I prepared to handle what goes along with this: going to the doctor alone, telling my parents, telling my partner, and/or having people find out about it through gossip?

- If I get pregnant or get someone pregnant am I prepared to handle this: telling my partner; telling my parents; going to the doctor; deciding about an abortion, adoption, or parenting; and/or having people find out about it through gossip?

- Does this decision align with my spiritual or religious

beliefs?

- Will we be in a safe place?

- Will it be at a safe time?

Ultimately, the decision to have sex with someone should be entirely your choice. This isn't to say you shouldn't consider your partner's feelings or desires, but you need to believe with your whole heart that this is the right person and the right time for you.

If you aren't truly ready, you may regret your choice. If your gut is telling you to wait, then pay attention to it. You will have plenty of opportunities in your lifetime to have sex, but only one opportunity to do it for the first time.

If you are pressuring your partner to have sex because you believe *you* are truly ready, then you aren't "truly" ready to have sex. Pressure should not be part of the equation here, from either person's point of view.

The first time should be a mutual decision, hopefully based on love and respect for each other. Pressuring someone isn't respectful or mature. Put yourself in their shoes for a minute. How does it feel to be pressured to do something you aren't ready for or don't want to do?

If you can't tell your boyfriend or girlfriend how you are feeling, what you need/want from them and the relationship, then you probably aren't ready for moving on physically. This goes back to the ideas of trust and communication.

Having sex with someone can change your relationship. It can become deeper and closer or cause a feeling of distance, all depending upon what your true feelings for one another are. Are you ready for your relationship to change?

Pressure!

Pressure can come from several different sources—your friends, your partner, the media, or yourself. Pressure can sound like this:

"Just get it over with!"

"It's not that big of a deal."

"If you loved me you would sleep with me."

If I have sex with him/her, he'll love me more/never leave me.

I'll be much cooler if I'm not a virgin.

We've been dating for X number of weeks/months/years, it's time for sex!

All my friends have had sex, I need to keep up with them.

"If you don't have sex with me, I'll leave you."

"If you don't continue to have sex with me, I'll leave you."

He'll/She'll leave me if I don't do it.

"So-and-so is doing it, you should too."

"It will strengthen our relationship."

"No one will find out about this."

"Everyone is doing it!"

Bottom line? Sex should always be a zero pressure situation.

Not ready? Here's Some help.

If you are not ready to move forward with your physical relationship, here are some strategies to help you wait until you are ready. One general tip, if you are in a relationship, the more time you spend alone together, the more likely you will be to have sex before you are ready. When you're alone, it's easy to get carried away, so try to reduce the opportunities for this to happen[15].

Here are some ideas of things you can do that will help you wait until the time is just right:

- Talk about what you will and won't do physically.

- Be confident in your decision to wait. Having sex should never be a requirement in a relationship.

- Agree on a "safe word" and action (like grasping your partner's hands and pulling away). This is something either of you can say and do if you think you are going too far. It means, "stop now!" and can be more effective than just saying "no" or "stop."

- If you are being pressured, tell someone and ask them to help you deal with it—two brains work better than one.

- Make a list of snappy comebacks for when you're being pressured: "If you loved me, then you wouldn't be pressuring me to do something I'm not ready to do!"

- Go on double dates in public places.

- Find non-physical ways to show you care.

- Do things with each other's families (most parents like this, so consider this an opportunity to gain bonus points with them. Plus, they probably want to get to know your boyfriend or girlfriend anyway).

- Do an activity together like volunteering, hiking, biking, skating, seeing a movie, listening to music, playing video games, cooking, baking, or anything else you can think of.

- Talk about your hopes and dreams for the future. This helps to make your dreams become a reality and will help you make better choices about when to become sexually active.

As you can see, emotions play a big part in the decision to have sex. When you are able to deal with and talk about your emotions and your partner's emotions, it goes a long way to helping you be really ready for sex. Your goal should be to feel really great about your decision when you look back at your life and think about your choices about sex.

Stuff to Think About!

What stands out for you about these virginity loss tales? How have they influenced your thinking about having sex?

How can you respond to pressure to have sex? What could you say to your partner, friends or even yourself?

What are your plans for the future? How would they change if you became pregnant or got someone pregnant?

How emotionally ready are you for sex? What do you need to change for you to be really ready?

CHAPTER TWELVE

Are You Ready For Sex?
Part 2: The Physical Stuff (Mostly)

We've looked at some of the emotional things you should think about before you have sex and now it's time to consider the physical parts of being ready. No matter where you are on the ready-for-sex scale, there are some important things you need to consider.

Every teenager needs to know about birth control and how to prevent Sexually Transmitted Infections (STI) and HIV. Even if you are planning to wait until marriage, the more information you have the better off you will be.

Some people think providing this kind of information to teens is the same as giving them permission to have sex. Frankly, giving you information about how to protect yourself and your partner isn't going to make one bit of difference in your decision to have sex—people have sex whether or not they know how to use a condom, right? The difference is, people who know how to use a condom are more likely to use one and reduce their chance of pregnancy and getting an STI or HIV.

Here are some interesting facts that will show you what some people in your age group are dealing with:

- About 57 out of 1,000 US teen girls get pregnant each year. Hispanic or African American girls are three times more likely to become pregnant than white girls. Americans have one of the highest teen pregnancy rates in the developed world[16].

- In Holland, about 5 out of 1,000 teens give birth each year[17]. Just a little comparison with a culture (unlike ours) that provides tons of information to their kids and teens, is open about sexuality, being safe, and has easily accessible condoms and birth control.

- One in four teenage girls in the United States has an STI[18]. It stands to reason that a ton of boys have an STI too, since they are having sex with these girls. Think of four of your favorite friends and then do the math.

- Of the 19 million STI infections in the US each year, half are in people aged fifteen to nineteen[19]. Yippee! It's a germ fest out there.

- Many young adults became infected with HIV in their teen years. This is why it's so important to make condom use a regular part of your sex life from the beginning[20].

- The average age a teen has sexual intercourse for the first time is about seventeen. This does not mean you need to have sex by then. It just means that most teens have sex at that age. The rest do it earlier or later[21, 22].

How Do You Know Your Vagina Is Healthy?*

This may seem weird, but frankly, people (including adults) are often very confused about vaginas. I think one of the reasons we have such a high rate of STIs among young people is because they don't know when something is "up" down there and STI's don't always have visible symptoms.

Here are some vag factoids so you will know if yours is in good shape:

- Vaginas are self-cleaning. You don't need to douche because the natural secretions clean her right up. Douching (washing the inside of your vagina) can lead to infections so please, don't do it! Soap and water on the outside, nothing on the inside should keep her nice and clean.

- The outside of the vaginal area—where the opening to the vagina, the clitoris, the urethra, and the labia are— is called the vulva. This means "covering" in Latin.

- "If it's clear and white, it's alright. If it smells or is itchy, something's fishy". Nancy Redd says this about vaginal secretions in her great book, *Body Drama*[23].

- A healthy vagina secretes about a teaspoon of clear or whitish stuff every day. It shouldn't be chunky, yellow or green, and there shouldn't be a lot of it.

- A healthy vaginal area has no offensive smell. Everyone's smells different. It shouldn't be stinky, fishy, oniony, yeasty (like bread), cheesy, or really funky smelling in any way. If your vaginal area has any yucky smell at all, go see a healthcare provider. You may have an infection of some sort. And don't be embarrassed. Most often it's something called bacterial vaginosis (BV). BV needs to be treated with antibiotics, so if you suspect any kind of infection, see a healthcare provider.

- A healthy vulva and vagina are not inflamed, rashy, or red. Depending on your skin coloring, your vaginal area can be tan, brown, dark brown, pink, tannish pink, or brownish pink.

- A healthy vaginal area is not tender to the touch, irritated, raw, or burning. If you have sex for the first time it could hurt, because the vagina is being stretched and this can be uncomfortable, but this is only temporary.

- Your vagina and vulva shouldn't be itchy. If it is, you may have a yeast infection and you can treat this over the counter, but it's better to check with your healthcare provider, especially if you've been sexually active at all.

- If you have any burning or trouble peeing, get checked out. This may mean you have a bladder infection, which doesn't have anything to do with your vagina, but I needed to mention it, so here it is.

If you are at all concerned that something's wrong "down there," tell your parent or a trusted friend and go see a healthcare provider. It's the smart thing to do.

Guys, you need to read this too! To be a good partner, you should know when to worry about your gal's vagina and be able to talk to her about it if you are worried.

How Do You Know Your Penis Is Healthy?*

Penises are less mysterious than vaginas, as they are all out in the open and much easier to see. In the interest of fairness, I thought I'd provide some tips about what a healthy penis looks like. By the way, STI's don't always have visible symptoms—so it's better to be safe when you have sex and use a condom. Every time.

Some penis (and testicle) factoids:

- Penises come in all different shapes and sizes. Long, short, fat, skinny—it's all normal. Some curve when they're erect and this is normal, too.

- Most penises are about the same size when erect. So

that guy you noticed in the locker room with the gigantic penis? It won't get much bigger when it's erect.

- Random acts of senseless erections are normal in adolescence. He'll calm down.

- Some guys are circumcised—this means the foreskin (this is skin that slides up and covers the head of the penis) was removed when they were babies. Some guys are not circumcised. Both are normal.

- A healthy penis doesn't have any sores, scabs, or raw spots.

- A healthy penis doesn't have any bumps that look flat, white or pinkish; blisters; or clusters of little bumps. It might have some wrinkles, blood vessels, pubic hair, or the occasional ingrown hair (this looks like a pimple sometimes).

- Generally, penises don't have much smell. If your penis smells fishy or funky, even after you wash, you may have a bacterial infection. See your healthcare provider. This is usually more of a concern for uncircumcised penises.

- If you have any burning or trouble peeing, get checked out.

- Your testicles or balls may be small or large or medium sized and one might be bigger than the other. If they swell or you have a lump of any sort, see your healthcare provider.

As with our friend the vagina, if there is anything at all funky with your parts, go see a healthcare provider. It's the smart thing to do.

Girls, you need to read this too! To be a good partner, you should know when to worry about your guy's penis and be able to talk to him about it if you are worried.

STIs and HIV (and Some Info That Might Freak Out Your Parents)

If you think you have an STI, call your doctor or a clinic, tell your parents or a friend and get some medical help. Left untreated, STIs can cause trouble later in life, like problems getting pregnant, pelvic inflammatory disease, embarrassment, or even death (thank you, Mr. HIV). You cannot tell by looking at someone if they have an STI, so it's important to talk about it and get tested before you have sex with someone.

What's "Safer Sex"?

Safer sex means sexual activity that does not involve any exchange of body fluids—semen, vaginal secretions, or blood. Kissing, touching, sexual talk, masturbating alone or at the same time, phone sex, mutual sexting, sex with a condom, and sex within a mutually monogamous (no other partners) relationship are examples of safer sex activities.

You can get STIs from anal and oral sex, so it's important to use a condom when you do either of these things. A guy won't notice much of a difference if you use a condom when you perform oral sex (especially if you spit in the condom before it goes on). This simple precaution will keep you from getting HIV, herpes, HPV (warts) or gonorrhea in your throat or mouth.

If you are planning to perform oral sex on a girl, you should use some sort of a barrier so you don't get any of the aforementioned infections in your mouth. Plastic wrap, you know, the stuff sandwiches come wrapped in, is a great barrier. It's wide, thin and won't really impact her pleasure at all.

Use a lot of lubricant if you plan on having anal sex because the chance of the condom breaking is much higher and this is one of the easiest ways to get HIV. And take your time if you decide to have anal sex—slower is better because it can be painful if not done correctly and carefully.

Talk about using protection with your partner even if it feels a little weird or uncomfortable. It's much weirder and more uncomfortable to tell someone you have an STI. Always re-member: safer sex is better sex because you won't worry (as much) about getting pregnant or an infection.

If you are already sexually active and on some form of birth control, condom use is still an absolute must. As I'm sure you know, birth control (like the pill) doesn't protect against get-ting an STI. It does not mean you are loose, dirty, or anything else if you take care of your sexual health. It just means you are smart enough to want to make sure nothing happens to either of you.

A small percentage of people are allergic to latex. If you use a condom and then experience burning or a rash immediately afterwards, this could be because you are sensitive to latex. Non-latex condoms are available, but do not use lambskin condoms, they don't prevent STI transmission. You can find polyurethane and other types of non-latex condoms at the drug store.

What if your partner doesn't want to use a condom? Unless you've been dating for a year, have been tested and you both have no other partners, condoms should be a requirement. If your partner "doesn't like them" there are tons of different kinds, so some thing is bound to work. Also, if you spit in the condom, or put a tiny drop of lubricant or spermicide in it, it'll feel better.

You can make this fun by testing them out until you find the perfect fit. It really isn't worth it to risk an STI or pregnancy because you can't take the time to find something that works for both of you. Being sexually active is an adult decision and requires adult behavior.

Women, because of the way we are made, get infections more easily. Our vaginas are pretty tough, but because of the tender mucus membranes down there, we can get infections easily. The same goes for anal sex—because the colon is a mucus membrane, it's easy for it to get torn and infection to get in. Condoms, people. Condoms.

If you haven't already learned about the different types of STI's, it's time. The Planned Parenthood website has great information about how STI's are transmitted, treatment and symptoms.

Baby Away or Preg-NOT: Birth Control

Of course, you know that the best way not to get pregnant is to not have sex at all! But, as you also know, this method fails all the time. In fact, a girl has an 85% chance of getting pregnant if she does not use any birth control at all. Fortunately, there are tons of birth control methods that work really well[24, 25].

These days, hormonal birth control is very safe and there are many different kinds so if you don't like one, there is bound to be another you will like. When the birth control pill was first introduced, its hormone dosages were high since scientists weren't sure about how much it would take to prevent a pregnancy.

Today, however, they really have it figured out, and even though it might take a few months for a girl's body to adjust to a hormonal method, there is most likely a pill, patch, ring, or rod that will work for you and not give you unpleasant side effects. Avoiding the most unpleasant side effect of them all—unplanned pregnancy—is just plain smart.

Your healthcare provider will help you find something that works for you and your body. If you do have side effects that drive you crazy (extra bleeding, nausea, vomiting, or being super cranky) tell your healthcare provider. Of course, if you have a side effect that is dangerous (your healthcare provider will tell you what to watch out for), you need to stop taking the medication and call them immediately.

Barrier methods (they make a barrier so it's really hard for the sperm to reach the egg), like condoms, sponges, diaphragms and cervical caps are also easy to use and fairly effective. Also, a young woman can get an Inter Uterine Device (IUD), which is put inside her uterus and stays there for 3 to 5 years. It works by making the uterus a bad hostess for fertilized egg implantation.

One of the easiest to get and cheapest to use is a condoms and spermicide together[26].   Put a tiny amount of spermicide inside the condom before the guy puts it on. Don't use too much, however, because the condom can slip off. The spermicide zaps the sperm on its way out, so there's way less chance of pregnancy. Put some inside the vagina as well, just in case some semen leaks or the condom breaks.

The Planned Parenthood website is a great source of information about all the different types of birth control available, how effective they are, cost and how they are used. Go check it out and find something that you think you'd like to try.

A Rant About. . . . Emergency Contraception!

There is a lot of confusion about how Emergency Contraception (EC) or the "morning-after pill" works, so I thought I'd clear it up. If a woman has unprotected sex she can take pills with in five days that will prevent her from becoming pregnant. It works by keeping a woman's ovary from releasing an egg for longer than usual[27]. Pregnancy cannot happen if there is no egg to join with sperm.

The morning-after pill does NOT cause an abortion.

If she is already pregnant (an egg has been fertilized), the pregnancy will not end. EC is for emergencies—not for use as a regular birth control method. It's a high dose of hormones and sometimes girls feel a little nauseated when they take it. If you are sexually active, you can and should purchase EC at the drug store or ask your healthcare provider for some. This way you have it available immediately in case you or a friend needs it.

You're Pregnant! She's Pregnant!

Teen pregnancy is something every teen girl thinks about and most teen guys consider, too. It's a big deal to become pregnant when you are a teenager. The idea of this may not seem real to you, which makes it easy to think, "It won't happen to me." But it might. Seriously. Did you read those pregnancy statistics?

You may even know someone who is pregnant right now. It's smarter to think: "It might happen to me" and take steps to prevent an unplanned pregnancy. You know, of course, the best way to prevent a pregnancy is to not have sex at all. Obviously, this doesn't apply to those of you in same-sex relationships. You might want to think through the questions below anyway, because they could be helpful to you if you have a friend who is going through something like this.

Pregnancy and lifetime companion STIs like herpes or HIV are two of the biggest consequences of having sex. Also, sex can change everything in your relationship. You may know this already, or ask any one of your friends who've had sex and they will probably tell you the same thing. Once you have sex, it's very hard to go back to the way things were before, especially if you are in a relationship.

Do yourself a favor and spend some time seriously thinking through the following questions. And if you have a boy- or girlfriend, chat with them about these issues, too. It's important to know where they stand. If you're gay or only have sex with someone of the same sex, it's important for you to think about this too. You can be a better help to your friends if they need you.

- How would your life change if you were involved in a pregnancy?

- Parenting: What would you do if you wanted to parent and your partner didn't want to? What would your plan be?

- Adoption: If you're a girl, what would you do if your boyfriend was pressuring you to give the baby up for adoption and you didn't want to? If you're a guy, what would you do if your girlfriend wanted to give the baby up for adoption and you didn't want to?

- Abortion: If you are a guy, what would you do if your girlfriend decided to have an abortion, but you don't believe in it? If you're a girl, what would you do if your boyfriend was pressuring you to have an abortion and you didn't want to?

This sex stuff is serious business! We've looked at the emotional side of sex and now we've covered the physical side. The more prepared you are, the better it will be when the time comes. I want you to have a great experience when you have sex for the first time and every time after—but more than that, I want you to have a safe time and feel really confident, informed and truly prepared for this big step into adulthood. When you tell your virginity loss story, my hope is you will have no regrets. And if you've already lost your virginity, my hope is your next sexual relationship will be tons better.

Stuff to Think About!

What do you think about the statistics from the beginning of the chapter? If you think "This won't happen to me?" what's your plan to make this come true?

If your partner doesn't want to use a condom, what can you say to them?

What would you do if you thought you had an STI or were diagnosed with one? How would you tell your partner?

All that pregnancy and STI stuff can be kind of a downer. After reading about this, how has your view of sex changed?

CHAPTER THIRTEEN

Your Rules! What It Takes to Date You

Okay, you've made it through a fake date, learned about different situations that can come up, understand what a healthy relationship looks like, and know all about birth control and STIs. There is a lot that goes on before, during, and after a date. One way to make your dating and romantic life easier is to develop a list of rules or guidelines for dating you. These will help you stay true to yourself and your values, and decrease the chance of ending up in a risky situation.

All the uncertainty that can come along with going on a date with someone new, falling in love, breaking up, having sex (or not) continues to happen as you get older and date more people. No one ever really gets over it. You just get used to it and know to expect feeling some nervousness before you go out with someone new the first few times. You understand the process, so it gets easier.

If you develop a personal list of rules for dating you, you will feel more confident and comfortable getting to know someone in a romantic way—or deciding they aren't the guy or girl for you. By providing yourself some structure, it makes it easier to stand your ground if you need to, dump someone, or survive being dumped.

You probably won't always stick to these rules and most likely, they will change, but going through this process will help you in the long run. It's important to write down your rules and be clear about what they mean. Clarity is powerful because it helps keep things—your goals and dreams, for example—in focus.

Most adults don't give dating much thought and just wing it, so consider yourself ahead of the game because you've been smart enough to take a little time with this. Adults get into dating messes more often than they'd care to admit, which may explain our high rate of divorce and all the relationship advice books and websites out there.

I've provided some points to think about and questions to answer that I hope will help you get pretty darned smart about you and your dating life. At the end, you'll have an opportunity to make a list of your top five rules for dating you.

How Will You Know When You Are Ready for Dating?

When you are out with someone there is a certain amount of risk, both emotionally and physically, so you need to be prepared to handle whatever may come your way. The following is a bunch of stuff to think about that will help you be ready before you head out the door with your über-crush.

Handy-dandy Dating Rules Checklists and Quiz

Confidence, limits, relationships and communicating—this list will help you figure out your strengths in these areas. If you can't say "Heck yeah!" to some of these, make a note and think about what will turn your "no" or "sorta" into a confident "yes!" Some will be easy to figure out, some will be a little more challenging. Practice the tougher ones like "saying no" with your close friends and family when they ask you to do something you don't want to do so you can see how they re-spond. No one will die. I promise.

Answer yes, no or sorta to the following:

- I can confidently say "no" to things I don't like or don't want to do.

- I can express my thoughts and opinions clearly.

- I communicate with my parents (most of the time) so they know where I am, what I'm doing and who I'm with.

- I follow through when I make a commitment.

- I can and will ask for help if I need it and know who to ask.

- I am clear about when I plan to become sexually active.

- I am comfortable talking about birth control and STI/HIV prevention.

- I have thought through how far I will go physically.

- I know what a healthy relationship looks like and know the signs of trouble.

- If my date says "no" I will totally respect their wishes without whining, pressuring or threatening.

- I know how to use public transportation, call a taxi, etc. if I need to.

- I know myself, my values, and what's important for me.

- I trust my instincts.

- I have clear goals for my future.

- I have an escape plan in place.

- I will definitely know if my date is being disrespectful of me.

Here's a list of different physical things you could do in a relationship. Think about how far you are willing to go and think about what you'd do early in the relationship vs. what you'd do later (like after a year). What is your limit?

- Shake hands

- Hold hands

- Hug

- Kiss

- Make out

- Make out like a maniac

- Be touched over clothes

- Be touched under clothes

- Touch privates over clothes

- Touch privates under clothes

- Masturbate together

- Give/receive oral sex

- Get naked together

- Have vaginal sex

- Have anal sex

Just a note of caution—you may feel really confident about how far you will go right now, in this moment, as you are thinking about all of this. The reality is that it's very hard to stick to your limits when you are messing around with someone. It feels good, you're having fun and, well, one thing can lead to another and you find yourself naked!

It's smart to be really clear with your partner about your limits before things get hot and heavy. Another tip is to stick to situations that make it harder for you to have opportunities to fool around.

POP QUIZ!

Feel free to use a separate piece of paper to record your answers.

True or False:

- I think guys should ask girls out and not the other way around.

- I am comfortable splitting the bill.

- I am comfortable telling my date if I am uncomfortable or don't want to do what they want to do.

- I think oral sex is no big deal.

- I think anal sex is no big deal.

- I think having sex before you get married is okay.

- I am planning to wait until marriage before I have sex.

- I know all about birth control, where to get it, and how to use it.

- I understand how STI's and HIV are transmitted and what to do to prevent transmission.

- You can tell by looking at someone that they have an STI.

- You can tell by looking at someone that they are straight, gay, lesbian, or transgender.

- I think being gay or lesbian is wrong.

- I think being gay or lesbian is just another way of being human.

- I have more than one trustworthy adult to confide in if I have problems.

- My boy- or girlfriend's values are similar to mine.

- My religion is very important to me.

- My parents trust me.

- I trust my parents to do what's best for me.

- I trust myself to make great decisions.

This quiz is merely intended to help you think more about your values and beliefs about dating, relationships and sexuality. Everything in the quiz is something you will be confronted with—whether it's your belief about being gay, how trustworthy your parents are, or some of things that may come up when you are on a date.

Parents and Dating

Perhaps you already have some dating rules provided by your parents. While annoying, this is also great. It shows they care about you and want you to be successful in your love life. They probably don't want you to make the same mistakes they (or their parents) did.

It may also seem like they don't want you to have a love life because the rules seem over-the-top restrictive—like they don't trust you to make good and safe decisions. There may be an element of truth to this. You know how it freaks you out to think about your parents involved in anything romantic? They probably feel the same way about you, but for different reasons. They remember all the mistakes they made and the stories they heard and they want you to do better!

Just because you are going to make a list of your own personal rules for dating you, it doesn't mean that you get to ignore the rules your family already has in place. Actually, you may be able to get some of your parents rules loosened up if you show your parents you can play by their rules, are trustworthy, and respect their seemingly stupid decisions.

Your rules for dating you are to keep you emotionally and physically safe. Your family rules are too, but in a more general sense. For example, they don't want you out and about in the wee hours of the night. They know from personal experience that all kinds of trouble can brew when it's late!

What Are Your Rules?

What's your bottom line, what are your deal breakers? Spend some time thinking about this be-cause it will serve as a road map for you as you move through your dating life. Your rules may even change over time. Just be sure you feel great about your choices. If your intuition tells you something isn't right, it's not. Trust your gut and stick to your top five rules and you'll become an expert dater in no time.

Remember, the people you are dating may have some of their own rules. It's important you respect their choices and boundaries, even if you don't agree with them or think they are silly. If you find yourself in a situation where you are tempted to break one of your hard and fast rules, this might be an indication that the person you are dating isn't "the one" for you. Bottom line; treat your date the same way you want to be treated.

Here some rules you might consider:

- Any sign of any "red flag" behavior and that's the end of the date.

- I will not have sex until I have the discussed two most important things: how we feel about each other and

145

what this means for our relationship.

- My religious beliefs need to be shared by my date.

- My parents will know who I'm with, where we're going and when I'll be home.

- My intuition is my friend – if I feel uncomfortable in any way, I will pay attention!

Your turn! On a separate piece of paper, write down your top five or 10 rules for dating you!

Stuff to Think About!

According to the checklists, how ready are you for dating? What areas do you need to work on?

What are the rules for dating in your family? If you don't have any, list some of your friends' family rules.

What was it like to really think about your dating rules? Any surprises?

CHAPTER FOURTEEN

A Few Final Thoughts!

Here are a few questions from the pop quiz from the introduction. Take it again and see what's changed!

I feel confident and excited about dating and starting a romance.

I am ready for a sexual relationship.

I know and have thought about the qualities that are important to me in a boyfriend or girlfriend.

I know my own values about dating, relationships, and sex.

I am clear about my limits and how far I'll go sexually with someone.

I know the signs of trouble in a romantic relationship.

I feel confident, smart, and ready for just about any dating situation.

Well, that's it! The rest really is up to you. Hopefully, after reading this book and thinking through all the questions, you feel stronger, smarter, better, happier, more confident, and all and all, significantly more prepared for the big, crazy, fun, maddening, eye-opening world of romance and dating. And sex too!

Your parents, friends, and other trusted people in your life want you to feel good about yourself, make great decisions and be a happy, healthy dater. If you need help, ask for it. There is no reason for you to travel this road alone.

Good luck out there!

About the Author

I bet you're wondering what makes me, a forty-plus-year-old, married, mother of one boy an expert on what you, a teenager, need to know about dating and sex. There're a few things. First, I was a teenager who did not know my sexual values. I had plenty of information about the facts and science of sex and sexuality, but little or no help when it came to dating, relationships, and sex.

I didn't have any kind of game plan, or anyone other than my friends (who were in the same boat) to actively guide me through this confusing period in life. I did have one adult friend who was helpful, and my friends were great, but as I look back, I realize they were busy haphazardly developing their own values and beliefs and were not the best guides for me.

I was a geeky, shy, awkward, braces-wearing, skinny, freckle-faced redhead who did not fit the stereotype of "pretty." My self-confidence wasn't very high, even though I had plenty of friends and was smart and funny. I had a seemingly endless number of crushes, but never had a boyfriend until I was out of high school. The crushes were fun but torturous, as I was too shy and lacking in confidence to ever say anything to any of them or do anything about it. By the time I was a sophomore in high school, it seemed (not true!) that every single one of my friends had a boyfriend, had sex, or both and I felt totally left out.

While I had a lot of practical information about sex, puberty, birth control, and sexually transmitted infections from books and my friends, I had little help when it came to handling my boyfriend-less state. I didn't understand my feelings of jealousy toward my friends, and I wasn't confident that it really was just fine that I didn't have a boyfriend and wasn't sexually active.

My two best friends made it seem like sex was no big deal (sound familiar anyone?) and even though I didn't have a boyfriend, they convinced me to "get it over with."

So I did.

Only when I finally fell in love for the first time, did I see what I'd been missing and how making that choice to "get it over with" wasn't the smartest thing I could have done. I didn't understand that waiting until I was "really" ready, instead of being pressured by my friends and myself, might have been smarter.

I'm sure my personal experience led me to my work throughout my twenties and thirties as a pregnancy and sexual health counselor in a variety of organizations. I have counseled nearly anyone you can think of about just about every aspect of sexuality—pregnancy, abortion, adoption, pregnancy, STI and HIV prevention, birth control, sexual practices, and safer sex.

I love to help people learn about this challenging part of life and am very comfortable discussing it with all kinds of people from different backgrounds and belief systems. I've seen the direct impact on teenagers when they don't take having sex seriously. It can be extremely hard—both emotionally and physically.

Now that I'm a parent, I get how hard this is for parents to talk about this with their kid, so I took my passion for sexual health education and turned it into a business called Birds + Bees + Kids®. I am a parent educator, which means I teach parents how to be better parents, and my focus is helping parents talk to their kids about sexuality, love, and relationships.

I know many parents can't, won't or don't talk to their kids about sex and relationships. I'm working hard to help them get over themselves. They often think "not my kid" or "school will handle it!" You and I both know these are often really excuses to avoid talking about something that feels uncomfortable. Don't get me wrong, I know many, many parents who do talk to their kids - and way too much, sometimes, at least from your perspective.

My hope is this book will provide you with more information - and maybe even all the information you ever get - on this topic. The decisions you make right now, as you are learning about love and sex, will stick with you for a really, really long time.

I want you to look back and think "I made great choices and feel really good about my first relationships and the first time I had sex." No regrets. And if I had a small part to play in this, well, I'd be a very happy woman.

Resources

Telephone hotlines (you can call anonymously):

Stop it Now! StopItNow.org

888.773. 8368

Help if you have been sexual abused or sexually abused someone.

Rape, Abuse and Incest National Network RAINN.org

800.656.4673

More sexual abuse or sexual violence help.

The National Domestic Violence Hotline

TheHotline.org

800.799.7233

Help if you are in a violent relationship or are worried about your relationship.

The Trevor Project

TheTrevorProject.org

866.488.7386

Crisis line for lesbian, gay, bisexual, transgender and questioning youth.

Websites

Values and Self-improvement

WikiHow.com - Search: "Define your personal values"

Spend a little more time learning about your values in general, not just as they relate to romance.

SelfCounseling.com - Go to "Personal Success"

You will find some fun and interesting things to do to help you become a better you!

Sexuality and Health

PlannedParenthood.org

One stop shopping for birth control and STI info.

AdvocatesForYouth.org

You'll find all kinds of information here, some related to sexuality, some not. They are a very active group which supports the rights of teens everywhere. It's worth a visit.

StayTeen.org

A great site sponsored by the National Campaign to Prevent Teen and Unplanned Pregnancy. Lots of articles, blogs, and videos covering relationships, sex, pregnancy, contraception, and abuse.

ScarletTeen.com

Tons of practical, easy to understand advice and information about sexuality, sex, STIs, being gay, you name it, it's here.

SexEtc.org

General information about sex and sexuality.

Lauras-Playground.com/teens.htm

Tons of information and support for gender fluid teens.

TeenAIDS.org

A charity called PeerCorps put this up. It's dedicated to preventing HIV infection in teens, and saving those who have it. Lots of Q&A pages, with peers giving common sense answers to teens' questions. It addresses all the issues about HIV infection, especially the sex-related ones!

Acne.org

Okay, not about sex, but acne is a self-esteem killer. This is a great site, run by a former acne sufferer who cured himself with over-the-counter preparations, and started up this Web site. Full of common sense advice, research updates, and support.

ItGetsBetter.org

Gay? Lesbian? Questioning? This is the place for you – tons of advice and support so you can feel great about who you are becoming.

MySistahs.org

To quote directly from their web site: "MySistahs is a Web site created by and for young women of color to provide information and offer support on sexual and reproductive health issues through education and advocacy." Lots of blogs and articles—all based on common sense. Lots of personal stories, too.

The Virginity Project - VirginityProject.Typepad.com

A great site from the UK. The woman who runs it has been collecting people's virginity stories. A good read.

AmplifyYourVoice.org

Amplify is an online community dedicated to sexual health, reproductive justice, and youth-led grassroots movement building. Go here if you are a teen of color, gay or questioning, or just want to see some change in the world of youth and sexuality.

Pornography Help and Information

ThroughTheFlame.org

A comprehensive site for those who want help with how much you view porn. Full of articles, blogs, resources, and forums. They are not affiliated with any religion, though there is (appropriately) a "Religion and Spirituality" section in the forum.

MakeLoveNotPorn.com

Compares what porn says about sex with what reality says. Totally worth a visit!

FightTheNewDrug.com

If you are worried about your relationship with porn, there is help here. Their philosophy is total abstinence is best – which I don't agree with, accept when it comes to teens and young adults.

Relationships and Advice

HeyJosh.com

Josh Shipp is a funny, practical guy with loads of advice to share with you about all kinds of things.

TeenAdvice.about.com

Solid, general advice about all things teen.

LoveIsRespect.org

Quizzes, tips, info and just what you need if you are worried about dating violence.

Books

Teenage Life and Relationships

The Teen's Guide to World Domination - Advice on Life, Liberty and the Pursuit of Awesomeness, Josh Shipp

How to Train Your Parents in 6 1/2 Days, Margit Crane

Chicken Soup for the Teenage Soul on Love and Friendship, Jack Canfield, Mark Victor Hansen, and Kimberly Kirberger

The 7 Habits Of Highly Effective Teens, Stephen Covey

The Guide: Managing Jerks, Recruiting Wingmen, and Attracting Who You Want, Rosalind Wiseman

I Am That Girl: How to Speak Your Truth, Discover Your Purpose, and #bethatgirl, Alexis Jones and Sophia Bush

Sexuality

It's Perfectly Normal! Changing Bodies, Growing Up, Sex and Sexual Health, Robie Harris and Michael Emberley

The "What's Happening to My Body?" Book for Girls, Lynda Madaras with Area Madaras

The "What's Happening to My Body?" Book for Boys, Lynda Madaras with Area Madaras

What's Going on Down There? Answers to Questions Boys Find Hard to Ask, Karen Gravelle with Nick and Chava Castro

Body Drama—Real Girls, Real Bodies, Real Issues, Real Answers, Nancy Redd

Spare Me 'The Talk' A Guy's Guide to Sex, Relationships and Growing Up, Jo Langford

End Notes

1. Adapted from Wurtele, S. K. and Miller-Perrin, C. L., Preventing Sexual Abuse. University of Nebraska Press, Lincoln, NE. 1992.

2. Kaiser Family Foundation, "Sexual Health of Adolescents and Young Adults in the United States." http://kff.org/womens-health-policy/fact-sheet/sexual-health-of-adolescents-and-young-adults-in-the-united-states/ (accessed 5/15/14).

3. Adapted from Wurtele, S. K. and Miller-Perrin, C. L., Preventing Sexual Abuse. University of Nebraska Press, Lincoln, NE. 1992.

4. American Psychological Association, "Sexual orientation and homosexuality." http://www.apa.org/helpcenter/sexual-orientation.aspx (accessed 5/15/14).

5. University of Illinois, Springfield, "Continuum of Human Sexuality." http://www.uis.edu/lgbtq/safezonesession-handouts/(accessed 5/15/14).

6. American Psychological Association, "Sexualization of Girls."
http://www.apa.org/pi/women/programs/girls/report.aspx (accessed 5/23/14).

7. The National Campaign to Prevent Teen and Unplanned Pregnancy, "That's What He Said—What Guys Think About Sex, Love, Contraception and Relationships." http://thenationalcampaign.org/resource/thats-what-he-said (accessed 7/3/14).

8. Cooper, D., "Signs of a Healthy Relationship." http://www.livestrong.com/ article/25776-signs-relationship/ (accessed 1/2/10).

9. Relationship Sculptures, Lee Williams, PhD, Professor, Marital and Family Therapy Program, University of San Diego, School of Leadership & Education Sciences, 5998 Alcala Park, San Diego, CA 92110. Used with permission.

10. Alabama Coalition Against Domestic Violence, "Dating Violence." http:// www.acadv.org/dating.html (accessed 7/5/14).

11. Asian Counseling Referral Service, The Eastside Teen Peer Advocate Program, in person conversation (1/27/10).

12. Adapted from Domestic Abuse Roundtable. "The Cycle Of Domestic Violence." http://www.domesticviolenceroundtable.org/domestic-violence-cycle.html (accessed 7/7/14).

13. Johnson, T., Understanding Children's Sexual Behaviors—What's Natural And Healthy. Institute on Violence, Abuse and Trauma, San Diego, CA. 2013.

14. Guttmacher Institute, "Facts on American Teens' Sexual and Reproductive Health." http://www.guttmacher.org/pubs/FB-ATSRH.html (accessed 6/22/14).

15. Pogany, S. Sex Smart—501 Reasons to Hold Off on Sex. Fairview Press, Minneapolis, MN. 1998.

16. Guttmacher Institute, "Facts on American Teens' Sexual and Reproductive Health." http://www.guttmacher.org/pubs/FB-ATSRH.html (accessed 6/22/14).

17. Dutch Daily News, "Dutch teen pregnancy rate among lowest in the world."
http://www.dutchdailynews.com/dutch-teen-pregnancy-rate-among-lowest-in-the-world/ (accessed 6/22/14).

18. Pediatrics, 2009;124;1505. "Prevalence of Sexually Transmitted Infections Among Female Adolescents Aged 14 to 19 in the United States."
http://pediatrics.aappublications.org/content/124/6/1505.full.html (accessed 6/12/14).

19. Center for Disease Control and Prevention. "Sexual Risk Behavior: HIV, STD, & Teen Pregnancy Prevention."
lowest in the world."
http://www.dutchdailynews.com/dutch-teen-pregnancy-rate-among-lowest-in-the-world/ (accessed 6/22/14).

20. Centers for Disease Control and Prevention. HIV Surveillance Report, 2009 (2011). Volume 21. (accessed 7/7/14).

21. Guttmacher Institute, "Facts on American Teens' Sexual and Reproductive Health."
http://www.guttmacher.org/pubs/FB-ATSRH.html (accessed 6/14/14).

22. Advocates for Youth, "Adolescent Sexual Health in Europe and the U.S."
http://www.advocatesforyouth.org/publications/419-adolescent-sexual-health-in-europe-and-the-us (accessed 7/1/14).

23. Redd, N., Body Drama—Real Girls, Real Bodies, Real Issues, Real Answers. Gotham, New York, NY. 2007, pg 128.

24. Brown University Health Education, "Safer Sex & Contracep-tives General Information." http://www.brown.edu/Student_Services/Health_Services/Health_Education/sexual_health/safer_sex_and_contraceptives/safer_sex.php (accessed 6/14/10).

25. UC Davis Student Health Services, "Failure Rates of Birth Control Method." http://healthcenter.ucdavis.edu/topics/contraception/efficacy.html (accessed /5/10).

26. Kestelman P., Trussell, J., "Efficacy of the Simultaneous Use of Condoms and Spermicides." http://www.jstor.org/discover/10.2307/2135759?uid=3739416&uid=2&uid=3737720&uid=4&sid=21104434703553 (accessed 6/19/14).

27. Planned Parenthood. "The Morning-After Pill (Emergency Contraception)." http://www.plannedparenthood.org/health-info/birth-control/morning-after-pill-emergency-contraception#sthash.PdyIHp1f.dpuf (accessed 7/10/14.)

CPSIA information can be obtained
at www.ICGtesting.com
Printed in the USA
LVOW12s2301050516
486936LV00014B/200/P